Proudly supported by

BERLINER DOM
CITY-TOURS

Sissel Hansen / Startup Guide

Since we launched our first book in Berlin in 2014, the city's startup scene has seen incredible growth and become increasingly attractive to international entrepreneurs and investors.

In 2017, Berlin startups received the most funding in Germany, accounting for 69 percent of total funding, as reported by Handelsblatt. The same year, Berlin-based food-delivery service Delivery Hero and meal-kit startup HelloFresh both went public, cumulatively raising $1.4 billion through the IPOs, according to a report by consultancy firm EY. Not only that, the city has become a hotspot for innovation hubs, including those launched by the likes of Lufthansa, Daimler Fleetboard, Vießmann, Porsche and Deutsche Bahn. Google has also set its eyes on the city for a new campus.

One thing is clear: Berlin is changing, and fast. Fueled by Brexit, the city has seen a spike in international interest in recent years. As a result, its population is becoming more diverse and its startup scene is maturing. Although the German capital has long been known for its affordable rents and bohemian flair, rents are rising rapidly, and gentrification is slowly taking hold of the city. However, compared with other major cities like London, New York, Paris and San Francisco, living costs are still relatively low while standards of living remain high. Despite the city's changing face, there's still something in the air that feels freer, more experimental and less conventional than in other major capitals around the world.

With its vibrant cultural scene, a flourishing entrepreneurial community, and talent continuing to pour in from abroad, Berlin is slowly shedding its juvenile "poor but sexy" reputation (made famous by former mayor Klaus Wowereit) and beginning to grow up. A new crop of growing companies, such as Clue, N26 and Contentful, are becoming the new poster children for Berlin startups, and they are ushering in a new era for the city's entrepreneurs. We're delighted to be back in the city to delve into the startup scene during such an exciting time.

Sissel Hansen
Founder and CEO of Startup Guide

Ramona Pop / Berlin's Senator for Economics, Energy and Public Enterprises

Berlin is a diverse, young, innovative and international city with a vibrant digital economy and a unique and growing startup ecosystem. Berlin has become a byword for a new entrepreneurial spirit and a young-at-heart outlook that embraces change, particularly in the field of digital technologies. This open-mindedness is Berlin's unique selling point – also when it comes to startups.

Every city in the world tries to nurture and attract talent – as well as capital and infrastructure – to enhance the chances of a better and more sustainable future for its citizens. Every startup ecosystem wants to foster local and global connectedness, as well as testbeds and pilot applications. Berlin does this, too, in various activities like the Digital Hub Initiative. Berlin's Investment Bank also has a large variety of supporting programs, while IBB venture capital company "IBB Beteiligungs-gesellschaft" has invested – together with its partners – over €1.33 billion in recent years. Another example, among many, is the Berlin Startup Stipend, to which the state of Berlin and the European Social Fund contribute nearly €40 million.

Berlin is doing a good job: it ranks among the top ten startup ecosystems worldwide. We merge tolerance with talent and technology – and add some techno, culture, and creativity.

All of this helps Berlin to create a sustainable future, to build new industries, and to attract people. One-fifth of Berlin startups have relocated from other areas, which is the highest percentage worldwide.

Be sure to take part in the Berlin journey – you are very welcome to "Be Berlin!"

Ramona Pop

Local Ecosystem

[Facts & Figures]

- In 2017, German startups had a record year of investment with an increase of 88 percent to €4.3 billion. Berlin-based startups received 70 percent of this total investment, cementing Berlin as one of the most prolific startup scenes of Europe.
- Berlin has the highest percentage of female founders (16.2 percent) of any German city.
- People from about 190 countries call Berlin home and make this city a truly international metropolis.
- There are approximately 628,000 foreigners registered as living in Berlin at the end of 2016.
- 18.4 percent of the population is foreign-born, with most of these residents coming from Turkey, Poland, and Syria.
- Berlin has over 300 public and private research institutes offering incredible access to talent and scientific knowledge.
- Berlin's infrastructure offers office space at reasonable prices and a large array of technology centers and business incubators as well as more coworking spaces than anywhere else in Germany.

[Notable Startup Activity]

- Delivery Hero received €387 million investment round in 2017.
- HelloFresh received €268 million in its IPO.
- Auto1, an online used car marketplace, raised €360 million investment.
- Comtravo, an artificial intelligence technology that promises to simplify business travel, closed a Series A round with €8.5 million.
- Caspar Health raised €2 million to aid in further expanding their rehabilitation platform and venturing into Asia.

Sources: Ft.com, Berlin-Brandenburg office of statistics, Deutschland Startup Monitor 2017, ey.com, gruenderszene.com, businesslocationcenter.de

[City]

Berlin, Germany

[Statistics:]

Urban population: **3.7 million**
Metropolitan population: **6 million**
Area: **891.7 km2**
GDP: **€130 billion**

STARTUP GUIDE BERLIN

Local Community Partner / Silicon Allee

Berlin is the international startup capital of Europe. We're battling (and winning) against London in terms of venture capital invested in our local companies, and scaling global companies in every tech sector. While it may seem like Berlin's success happened overnight, the foundations were laid long ago. Berlin's history as a creative and experimental cultural capital started in the Weimar Republic and has taken many forms: theater, jazz, punk rock, street art, electronic music and now technology. It's this deep creativity and welcoming community that sets Berlin apart.

What hits home for us, as an organization founded by international immigrants, is the ability to arrive in Berlin and get settled in relatively easily (especially compared with our home country of the US). The historic open borders policy creates an amazing, diverse and international startup scene. Around 50 percent of all tech employees and a quarter of tech founders in Berlin are non-German, meaning you can find jobs, cofounders, and investment almost entirely in English (you'll need German friends to navigate the bureaucracy, but that's slowly changing too).

Silicon Allee sees its role as the embassy to this international tech community, and more specifically Berlin's central innovation district. Our services have evolved over the years but our mission remains the same: to connect Berlin's startups with the rest of the world. We've always been driven by the needs of our community and how to serve them better, whether that means publishing news, producing events, consulting companies moving to Berlin, touring international delegations, lobbying government officials or housing startups and entrepreneurs in our Berlin campus. Helping and giving first to this network of like-minded people is paramount.

It's this strong international network that aligned us with Factory.co and also why publications like Startup Guide, a road map to starting and expanding a professional network in any city, are so important. Since Silicon Allee interacts with so many international organizations, we also see publications like Startup Guide as vital diplomatic tools, allowing visitors from Japan, the US, the Middle East or Africa to send a bit of Berlin home to share with others.

Silicon Allee is happy to be part of this publication and excited to see Berlin continue growing its international network, influencing startup cultures around the world with its creativity, open-mindedness and passion. Welcome to Berlin, and Hello World!

Travis Todd, CEO and Cofounder
Andrew Haw, Community Lead
Florin Chici, Events Lead
The R/D Coffee Bar Team

cont

STARTUP GUIDE BERLIN

startups

programs

ents

spaces

experts

founders

Intro to the City

Berlin has been described as the city that's always becoming and never being, and it's certainly had a busy few decades. In the time since East and West Germany reunited in 1990, Berlin's become a political powerhouse, an artistic hub and a nightlife mecca – and, most recently, one of Europe's most vibrant tech and entrepreneurial ecosystems. The city's central location makes it a perfect jumping-off point if your company dreams of someday conquering Europe, and its high quality of life and relaxed atmosphere means you'll have fun along the way. Silicon Valley may have more money, but David Bowie never had a San Fransisco period.

Before You Come

Germany is known for its bureaucracy, and it's a reputation that's well earned. To avoid running into stress once you're in the country, you'll want to check off a few boxes before you arrive. First, you should start looking for apartments. Places are scarce in some of Berlin's trendier neighborhoods, but you'll need a permanent address to get started on all your other paperwork – and you've got a lot of it ahead of you. If you're planning on staying in Germany long term, you'll need an address to register at one of Berlin's *Bürgerämter* (municipal administrative offices) within two weeks of arriving. If you're subletting or living with a friend, you can use that residence with your landlord's written permission. (Pro tip: you can go to any Bürgeramt in the city, not just the one in your neighborhood; and you can often find an appointment much earlier if you're willing to take a half-hour trip to one of the less frequented offices in the suburbs.) You'll also want to make sure you have health insurance that meets German requirements. Whether you go with the public system or a private provider, you'll need to show a current policy when you apply for your visa.

Cost of Living

Berlin's unofficial motto is *"arm aber sexy"* ("poor but sexy"), and although the city has become more expensive recently, it's still relatively cheap compared with other major European cities. Many Berliners live in shared flats, and you can usually find a room in one for no more than €600, including utilities. You'll pay more for your own space, but there are still nice single-room apartments in popular neighborhoods for under €800. A meal in an average casual restaurant shouldn't set you back more than €15, and you can get groceries for about €50 per week. A monthly travel pass that covers all public transportation within the city (though not some of the farther-flung suburbs) will cost you about €80. Berlin also has a thriving bike culture if you'd prefer to bike. All told, you can live quite comfortably on €1,200 per month, and downright decadently on €1,500 or more.

Keep in mind, though, that while German taxes aren't as high as, say, Scandinavian taxes, you should expect to pay a significant portion of your income – up to 50 percent if you're a high earner. And you're legally obligated to have health insurance, which can add another €300 per month if you're paying for yourself.

INER
GALERIA

Cultural Differences

If you're coming from an English-speaking country, Germans in general – and Berliners in particular – may seem surprisingly... direct. Berliners are proud of their *Berliner Schnauze*, a mix of irreverence and bluntness that can come off as rude if you aren't used to it. Bus drivers in Berlin have little patience for questions, and woe unto the pedestrian who unknowingly occupies a bike lane. But once you've adjusted, you may come to appreciate the German style of communication. Germans tend to be sincere in their friendships. They generally prefer straightforward conversation to small talk, and their plans are sacred, not tentative.

Berlin's irreverence stems from its deep informality. You'll find that a pair of jeans is appropriate attire in 90 percent of offices, and that many Friday afternoons end with a beer with your coworkers. Germans also take pride in their work–life balance, which includes a generous amount of vacation time. Chancellor Merkel herself is frequently spotted hiking during the holidays, which she's entitled to as a government employee.

Renting an Apartment

Shared flats – called *Wohngemeinschaften*, or WG (pronounced "vay-gay" or "veh-geh") for short – are popular in Berlin, and you'll find many people well into their thirties who still live with roommates. You can often find a WG room for €300 to €600 per month. Rooms are listed on popular platforms like wg-gesucht.de or in Facebook groups such as Housing BERLIN or Wohnung und WG Berlin. You may have to go to a dreaded "WG casting call," however, to see if you're a good fit. Be prepared for something a bit like a job interview, except you may be asked about your cleanliness, music tastes, and cooking skills.

If you'd prefer your own place, you have two options: Many Berliners live as *Untermieter* (subletters) with arrangements varying in formality – and legality. You can often find a good deal if you don't mind moving again when your landlord needs the apartment back.
The alternative is to rent or buy your own flat, but you might face a few hurdles if you're not German. The local real estate market can be confusing and difficult to navigate for non-German speakers, and you'll need to produce a *Schufa*, a kind of credit check, before most landlords will consider you – and that can be tricky without a domestic financial record. But don't feel overwhelmed; there are many Berlin realtors who specialize in working with foreigners and who can help you find and be approved for your dream home.

See **Flats and Rentals** page **233**

RITÉ

Finding a Coworking Space

Berlin has a thriving ecosystem of digital nomads, and there are clusters of coworking spaces in several parts of the city. St. Oberholz near Rosenthaler Platz and Silicon Allee in Mitte are important hubs of Berlin's startup scene. Just one stop away in Prenzlauer Berg is Factory Berlin, a coworking space and incubator. Kreuzberg, the center of Berlin's hipster and artist scene, is home to the Berlin branch of the renowned betahaus. There are coffee shops all over the city, and reliable wifi available nearly everywhere. Note, however, that many cafes don't allow computers on weekends.

See **Spaces** page **78**

Insurance

Health insurance is mandatory for getting a visa, and you'll need time to figure out which plan is right for you, so make this a priority when planning your move. You have two main options: you can either enroll in the government-run public health insurance system or buy insurance from a private provider. Each has its pros and cons. The public insurance plans are more or less all-inclusive, so you should find all your expenses covered, including some benefits you may not expect. It can also be cheaper, as your monthly fee will be a percentage of your salary and is usually shared by your employer. Private insurance, meanwhile, often gets you faster service at doctors' offices, and you'll have more provider options. You may also end up paying less if you're younger and healthier. However, with some of the cheaper plans, you may also have to pay for some of your healthcare yourself; you unfortunately get what you pay for. That being said, all German health insurance plans have to meet certain government standards, so most will cover you in an emergency.

See **Insurance Companies** page **234**

Visas and Work Permits

If you're not from the EU, you'll need a permit to work or stay in the country at all for longer than ninety days. Fortunately, Germany has been taking steps to make its visa process more accessible, in part to foster the startup scene. And while it can be tedious, it isn't that difficult. If you're working for a company that's willing to sponsor you (or moving to Germany to take a job you've been offered), you'll need a contract or letter of intent from your employer specifying your start date. Freelancers need to produce a business plan showing your sources of income and your ability to support yourself, along with recommendations from clients attesting to your ability to find work. Ideally, you'll also have offers from prospective clients in Germany. In addition, you'll need to show proof of a current health insurance plan, a *Meldung* (registration of your living address), and an open bank account in Germany, along with any statements that show savings abroad. You can apply for a visa at a German consulate or embassy abroad, or at one of the *Ausländerbehörden* (foreigners registration offices) in Germany.

See **Important Government Offices** page **233**

Taxes

Hire an accountant. Seriously, even Germans are known to throw up their hands and seek professional help when faced with the complexity of their tax system, and they're fluent in the language. If you're moving to Germany for a full-time position and this is your only source of income, there is a chance you'll be able to manage your taxes yourself; but if you're a freelancer or investor, let alone founding your own company, you're better off hiring a *Steuerberater* (tax advisor) to take care of it for you, lest you find yourself filing incorrectly and paying a fine later.

Fortunately, there are many tax advisers in Berlin who cater to international clients and who can assist you in English and even help you interact with tax offices. And if you're a freelancer, their bills are tax-deductible – as are any other expenses that might conceivably be linked to your business, including transportation and training costs. So save those receipts.

See **Accountants** page **231**

Starting a Company

If you're looking to work as a freelancer, starting a company is easy. Once you've got your freelance visa, simply visit the *Finanzamt* (tax office) and fill out a form for your tax number. One thing to keep in mind, though: if you plan to make over €17,500 per year as a freelancer, you must charge your clients *Mehrwertsteuer* (value-added tax) and pass it along to the government. Your tax adviser will help with this.

To found an LLC (called a "GmbH" in Germany), you just need to show a notarized agreement between the various shareholders and investment capital of €25,000. Then you can enter your company into the *Handelsregister* (commercial register).

See **Programs** page **56**

Opening a Bank Account

You have a few major banks to choose from in Berlin, all of which have good branch and ATM coverage throughout the city. If you want a brick-and-mortar bank, there is Sparkasse, Volksbank, Deutsche Bank, Commerzbank or Postbank. They all offer roughly comparable benefits, allowing you to open an account and get a debit card that's accepted widely throughout Europe. To open an account, you'll need to bring your passport (with your visa) and address registration. Bank tellers may be reluctant to speak English, but they're usually helpful, especially if you bring a German-speaking friend. If you'd prefer an online bank, N26 and DKB are popular options. Both allow you to withdraw money from anywhere and manage your account online.

See **Banks** page **232**

U1 Warschauer Str 1 min

Getting Around

Berlin is an extremely well-connected city, and aside from the odd Ikea trip you'll rarely need a car. The S-Bahn and U-Bahn train services, along with a network of trams and buses, reach almost all parts of the city and are generally fast, reliable, and easy to navigate. Signs are in German and English, and maps are ubiquitous. A single €2.80 ticket provides access to all public transportation services within the central two zones of the city, or you can purchase a monthly pass for about €80, or less if you buy a year's worth at a time.

Berliners are passionate cyclists, and you should be able to find a new bike for about €200. With sizable bike lanes on nearly all roads and well-maintained paths cutting through public parks, it's often the fastest way to get around. There are maintenance shops all over town, and plentiful bike racks in public areas.

Phone and Internet

When you first arrive, you may want to get a prepaid phone plan to cover you for the first month or so. You can purchase phones with pre-installed SIM cards at all major electronic stores and most supermarkets. A phone with a month of credit shouldn't cost more than €20. Once you've got your German bank account set up and registered your apartment, you're ready to get a permanent phone plan. Whether you choose T-Mobile, O2, Vodafone or 1&1, you'll likely end up paying around €20–30 per month, depending on what kind of plan you need.

If you need to order internet for your home, one thing to know is German internet providers often take quite a while (sometimes up to a month) to connect a new customer. If you don't want to go a month without home internet, some providers offer the option of paying extra for an immediate hookup.

Learning the Language

German is a famously difficult language to learn, but it's not as bad as you've heard. If you're coming from an English-speaking country, you'll notice so many cognates that you'll be able to decipher a lot of signs and instructions right from the beginning; and if you speak a Romance language, you'll already have a handle on how to use the German cases. Either way, don't be afraid of making mistakes, as Germans often find the complexity of their language just as ridiculous as you do.

If you want to learn the language, there are many resources available in Berlin. There are language schools all over the city catering to students and young professionals, including the DeutschAkademie downtown, the deutSCHule in Neukölln and speakeasy in Friedrichshain, as well as Meetup and Facebook groups to find tandem partners. *Tagesschau*, Germany's public news broadcaster, produces daily news podcasts with slowly spoken German, and *Deutsche Welle*, Germany's public international broadcaster, publishes "simplified" news articles. If you're having trouble making progress in German, you'll also find that nearly everyone in Berlin speaks excellent English, and most signs will be bilingual. Just remember to bring a German friend with you to government offices.

See **Language Schools** page **235**

Meeting People

In part because of the startup scene, Berlin has a huge community of relatively new transplants and there are tons of ways to meet new people. Meetup.com lists dozens of events every day (in German, English and other languages) for interests ranging from physical fitness to meditation to board games. There's a particularly large number of programming Meetups if you're looking to make friends and network in the tech scene. To find more off-the-beaten-path events, check out the *Cee Cee* newsletter's Twitter feed and *Exberliner*'s magazine and website.

Berlin is also known as one of Europe's party capitals for a reason. There's a huge club scene with tourists traveling from around Europe for some of the more popular venues, and after you've spent some time in the city you'll find you're hearing about more gallery openings and house parties than you can possibly attend. And you won't even need to break your budget to enjoy yourself: a beer in one of Berlin's hipster bars usually costs less than €5, and you can enjoy a big night out at a club for less than €50, including late-night *Döner*.

See **Startup Events** page **235**

start:

ups

[Name]

assistr

[Elevator Pitch]

"We develop the technologies of tomorrow to help society care for the people that once cared for us. We develop technical solutions in the area of medicine, care and health tech."

[The Story]

Founder Jens Peter Grudno began assistr while taking part in the Berlin-based company-builder Next Big Thing. He worked differently from other participants by starting from the ground up: researching a problem to work with and then building a solution. "The global ratio of old to young people is going through a shift, and the amount of elderly people entering care homes will rise dramatically. When looking at the elderly-care market, we found one large problem area with practically no technical innovation: incontinence. This is not a sexy market to develop in, but I like this because of the unusually large potential to create real change, and it's a growing market where no one is doing anything in tech."

assistr's solution (the first in their goal to create elderly-care tech innovations "one breakthrough at a time") is intelligent incontinence pants linked to a cloud-based care infrastructure. The solution helps workers in elderly-care homes to plan their daily schedules better and evaluate needs. "Timing is critical to avoid diseases like urinary tract infections and pressure ulcers when patients are left unattended for too long," says Jens. "assistr's solution can optimize the daily care plans after just a few days of retrieving data, but also in a more immediate way where carers can change the order of who's seen first on an ad hoc basis, depending on the urgency of the situation."

[Funding History]

Seed

External

assistr received its first seed funding from Next Big Thing in 2017. This was followed by a pre–Series A round and then a second seed round from Die BrückenKöpfe in February 2018.

[Milestones]

- Getting our patents filed.
- Finishing our first demonstrator.
- Connecting with the five largest incontinence-pants producers in North America and Europe for collaboration.
- Establishing a clinical research partnership with Charité Hospital Berlin.

[Links]

Web: assistrcare.com

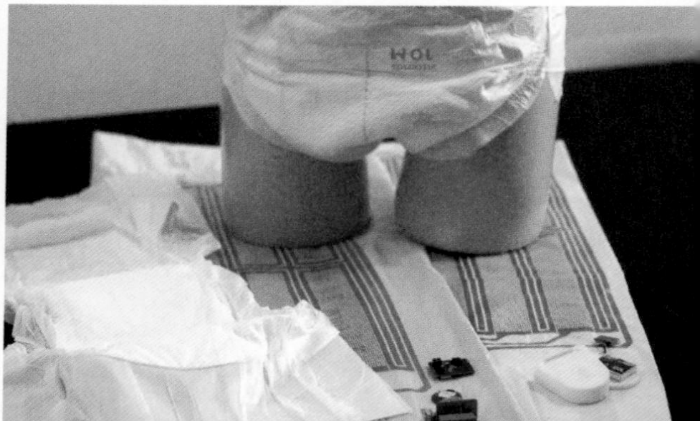

[Name]

BigchainDB

[Elevator Pitch]

"We help give people more power in a data economy."

[The Story]

BigchainDB had its beginnings in 2013 as a project between founders Bruce Pon, Trent McConaghy and Maria McConaghy. "We wanted to develop a system of intellectual property attribution using blockchain to solve the question of, 'How do the creators of any digital intellectual property get compensated?'" says CEO Bruce Pon. More specifically, they wanted to create a way for individuals to retain ownership of their digital art, which up until that point was a bit of a gray area. They created a service (ascribe.io) for artists and creators as a way to securely share and trace digital works. However, they quickly found out that many other sectors would also benefit from their innovation in controlling and transferring digital assets. So, in 2015, they formed BigchainDB. "With individuals and corporations from across all industries reaching out, looking to partner, collaborate, license or build on scalable blockchain technology," says Bruce, "it became clear that we were solving much more than our own problem. We give all creators the ability to claim their property in a borderless way."

BigchainDB supports sectors such as financial reconciliation, supply-chain logistics, health data and IoT without sacrificing scale, security or performance. Its solution allows developers and enterprise to "blockchainify" existing databases and infrastructures, with all of the blockchain perks, such as decentralization, transparency and stability, while also being highly secure with low latency.

[Funding History]

Bootstrap Seed Angel External

BigchainDB received €4.7 million in a Series A funding round over the course of four years, led by Earlybird Ventures but with additional support from Anthemis Group, RWE Ventures, innogy SE and Digital Currency Group.

[Milestones]

- **Founding the company.**
- **Releasing our first product ascribe.io in February 2015.**
- **Releasing the BigchainDB solution in 2016.**
- **Kicking off of Ocean Protocol in September 2017.**

[Links]

Web: **bigchaindb.com** Facebook: **BigchainDB** Twitter: **@BigchainDB**

SASKATCHEWAN

[Name]

Bunch

[Elevator Pitch]

We're a team management platform enabling high-growth companies to build, manage and scale organizational culture with workflow data, psychology and machine learning.

[The Story]

The team at Bunch, who refers to themselves as "workplace culture hackers," originally operated under the name of 12grapes as a project-based consultancy. "In 2016, we helped early-stage investors to evaluate a founder-team's dynamics," says CEO Darja Gutnick, "but after developing some prototypes for a software-based solution and a successful fundraising round, we rebranded under the name of Bunch." They decided to instead focus on working directly with companies and improving company culture from within. During the early stages of Bunch, Darja realized that a strong company culture is at the core of every successful team, and that adaptability can make or break a company as it goes forward.

Bunch helps fast-growing companies to build great teams. Each team member or new job applicant fills out a short online questionnaire based on the "Organizational Culture Profiling" method developed at Stanford University. Bunch then uses the data to create a culture profile for the company and each of its teams, focusing on the attributes Collaboration, Results-Orientation, Adaptability, Detail-Orientation, and Principles and Customer-Orientation. The profiles make it possible to predict, with a high degree of accuracy, the behavioral tendencies of individuals and teams in the organization. With this SaaS solution, team leaders can monitor progress, transparency and efficiency based on the pre-assessment and analysis of real-time communications (e.g., via a new Slack feature).

[Funding History]

Bootstrap Seed Angel External

Bunch raised its first angel round in the beginning of 2017. In April 2018, Bunch announced a larger funding round and is now backed by High Tech Gründerfonds, Atlantic Labs, MAKERS and Hyperion Invest.

[Milestones]

- Developing the world's first machine-learning model that predicts team culture from Slack data.
- Winning our first paid clients, thereby justifying the market.
- Raising our first early funding round.
- Achieving a 50/50 gender-mixed workforce in a high-pressure environment.

[Links] Web: bunch.ai Facebook: Bunch.aiHQ Twitter: @bunch_hq

bunch

[Name]

Codepan

[Elevator Pitch]

"We're an innovation lab developing a scalable general-purpose anomaly-detection tool called Streem.ai. It provides real-time analytics and helps discover abnormalities in vast amounts of data, turning them into valuable business insights."

[The Story]

Avi Elran and his cofounders Abou George and Gary Abela started Codepan in 2015 with a single mission: to create a safe place for great minds to flourish, imagine and build the products for the challenges of tomorrow. "During our early days of working in software development, the team realized that they wasted a lot of time and energy with failing APIs. This led to us on a search for a solution to identify these failures before they occur," says Avi. After two years of research and development, they came up with an anomaly-detection platform they named Streem.ai.

"Streem.ai is a tool that uses cutting-edge algorithms to identify issues and abnormalities in large amounts of data in real-time," Avi says. "With the increasing focus on IoT and Industry 4.0 resulting in exponential amounts of data being generated, our tool is the ideal personal AI assistant for engineers." Codepan is now a growing team of data scientists and software engineers and part of the latest Startup Autobahn Program. The founders consider it a great entry point into the automobile and manufacturing sector, where they're currently working on various pilot projects.

[Funding History]

Bootstrap

Codepan is 100 percent self-funded and bootstrapped. It plans to raise money soon to continue product development and push its product to market.

[Milestones]

- Releasing the first version of our own automated benchmarking system for Anomaly Detection.
- Getting selected into the Startup Autobahn Program.
- Signing our first paying client.
- Getting selected for an EXIST grant.

[Links] Web: codepan.com Twitter: @codepan_labs

[Name]

Coworkies

[Elevator Pitch]

"We're the first professional network for freelancers, startups, and small companies working out of coworking spaces. We help them connect and share experiences with other people in coworking spaces as well as identify work opportunities and events."

[The Story]

Appropriately enough, cofounders Pauline Roussel (CEO) and Dimitar Inchev (CPO) met at a coworking space in 2015. She was general manager of the space (called Rainmaking Loft at the time but since renamed The Place Berlin), and he was there as entrepreneur in residence at Startupbootcamp. "We noticed that members of the space generally faced the same issues," Pauline says. "They needed help with their accounting or taxes, or finding new employees, and they often missed networking opportunities." And while there was plenty of expertise among members of the city's many coworking spaces, the founders saw that there was almost no communication between them. Pauline and Dimitar decided to start a network that would act as the missing link to connect all these talented people. They began with intensive market research; then, after conducting a global survey to identify more common issues, they embarked on a journey themselves, visiting 283 coworking spaces in 30 cities around the world.

Based on their connections and feedback, they launched the alpha version of their platform in 2016. It included information on more than 450 coworking spaces. In 2017, they launched the beta version, which added an event directory and a job board where companies pay to advertise jobs. "When you're looking for help, there's usually someone perfect in a coworking space across town," Dimitar says. And Coworkies can help you find them.

[Funding History]

Bootstrap

Coworkies has been entirely bootstrapped. Even during their two-year research period, Pauline and Dimitar lived off their own money, focusing on really understanding the European coworking ecosystem before worrying about raising funds. Although both are "fully dedicated" to Coworkies and have no side jobs, they haven't yet sought out any seed funding.

[Milestones]

- **Visiting 283 coworking spaces in thirty cities as part of a two-year research mission.**
- **Launching the alpha version of the Coworkies websites in 2016.**
- **Getting the first two hundred coworking spaces to sign up to the platform.**
- **Launching the Coworkers job boards and acquiring customers.**

[Links]

Web: coworkies.com Facebook: coworkies Twitter: @Coworkies Instagram: coworkies

allbirds
STATION F
SWEET CHICK
Lovely Mornings!
Factory

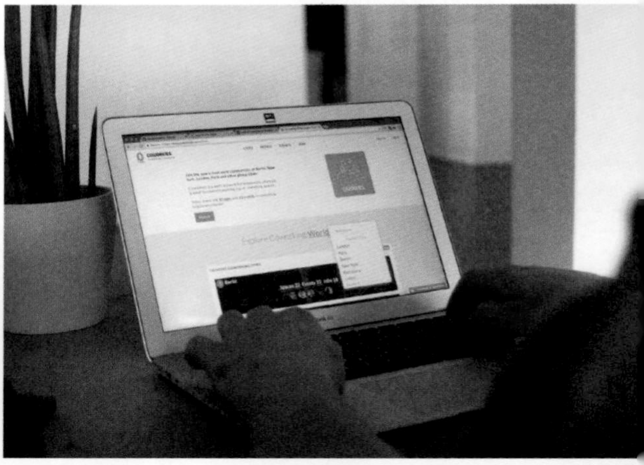

[Name]

GlassDollar

[Elevator Pitch]

"We're an investor-discovery tool for founders who'd rather be creating than wasting time on the fundraising process."

[The Story]

Fundraising is a crucial part of building a startup, but the process of finding investors can hamper progress, especially if the startups and investors don't end up being a good match. Cofounders Fabian Dudek and Jan Hoekman both had startup experience and knew firsthand how challenging it can be – both creatively and professionally – to find the right partnerships, so they launched GlassDollar at the end of 2017. GlassDollar's investor search engine allows startups to do away with the complicated process of sifting through investor lists. "We aggregate all of the investor lists out there," says Fabian, "and make it a lot easier for founders to focus on the most relevant investors for their company."

GlassDollar helps founders not only to find investors but also to get in contact with them. After sharing your pitch deck, you'll receive a list of investors whose criteria match with your startup. You confirm your preferred investors, and your pitch is shared with them. You'll then be directly introduced to the investors who showed interest. "Building something people love is hard," says Fabian. "Raising funds for it can make it even harder. We'll change that. If you're creating something people love, we'll make sure you have no problem raising funds for it."

[Funding History]

Bootstrap

GlassDollar has preferred not to be dependent on outside investors, so the founders bootstrapped and developed a default strategy that allowed them to get their startup off the ground and running without the need for investment.

[Milestones]

- Launching the investor search engine in late 2017.
- Getting voted into the top five of Product Hunt.
- Surpassing fifteen thousand investors on our investors database.
- Helping more than ten thousand founders discover investors.

[Links] Web: glassdollar.com Facebook: glassdollar Twitter: @glassdollar

[Name]

Green City Solutions

[Elevator Pitch]

"We've developed the CityTree, the world's first biotech filter to quantifiably improve air quality in urban habitats"

[The Story]

The CityTree combines plants with state-of-the-art IoT technology, creating a natural and intelligent air filter. Green City Solutions founders Dénes Honus, Liang Wu and Peter Sänger established the company in 2014 as a way of taking over and commercializing the results of ten years of research into air pollution. The CityTree is a four-meter-high stainless steel and aluminum structure with high-end IoT sensors and solar panels, and a carpet of moss covering each side. "Moss cultures have the ability to eat up pollution, are self-sustaining and don't need throwing away," says Dénes. The special moss cultures filter particulate matter and other harmful substances from the air, while innovative IoT technology measures the CityTree's environmental performance in real time and uploads the data to the cloud via proprietary software. The attached wooden benches offer passersby a place to take a break in the cleanest air in the city.

The CityTree has been installed in multiple locations in Germany and in European capitals such as London, Paris, Amsterdam and Oslo. It's a strong beginning for Green City Solutions, but Dénes and his colleagues aren't stopping there. "We want to have solutions for all aspects of city living, so in addition to the streets, we aim to expand to shopping facades and integrate into the ventilation systems of commercial buildings and private residences."

[Funding History]

Bootstrap

Seed

Green City Solutions spent the first two years self-financing the development and construction of its first prototypes. In 2016, it closed a pre-Series A seed round of €1.75 million.

[Milestones]

- Founding the company from a research project.
- Acquiring our first customer in April 2015.
- Successfully installing more than thirty CityTrees.
- Making the second generation of the CityTree available in May 2018.

[Links] Web: greencitysolutions.de Facebook: mygcs Twitter: @mycitytree Instagram: green_city_solutions

GREEN CITY SOLUTIONS
CityTree
IoT Lösung (Internet of Things)
GREEN CITY SOLUTIONS
getstarted

[Name]

Grover

[Elevator Pitch]

"We're a fresh alternative to owning things. We make technology accessible by enabling people to subscribe to tech products instead of buying them."

[The Story]

Grover have created their own niche in the consumer electronics field by offering a service where the latest brands and models of goods (such as cameras, smartphones, wearables and just about everything else) can be rented hassle-free and without any fixed-term obligations. When founder Michael Cassau returned to Berlin after time abroad, he intended to leave again soon after and didn't want to blow his cash by buying things outright or commit to any long-term financing plans. "I preferred to keep the money for travelling and experiences," he says. This inspired the idea for Grover, founded in 2015.

Consumer electronics is constantly being superseded, and this is another issue that Grover aims to address: they offer a flexible alternative to spending a lot of money on devices that will soon be outdated. Rentals are available either through the Grover website or through selected retailers direct from their product detail page. Losing track of payments can be a bit challenging in rental situations, but Grover has you covered. "We do have a purchase option at the end so people don't overpay," Michael says, "and there's an opportunity to purchase the item for €1 after you've paid three rental fees on top of the initial retail price." Grover has expanded its operations to New York, with plans to open into other locations in the States.

[Funding History]

Bootstrap Seed Angel External

Grover began the first ten months of operations in bootstrap mode to get a viable service ready for funding. It secured €1.3 million in late 2015 through a seed round and has since secured further investments through equity and asset-backed financing.

[Milestones]

- Receiving the venture funding in 2015.
- Setting up the asset-backed funding.
- Launching partnerships with a number of retailers (MediaMarkt, Saturn, Conrad, Tchibo and Gravis).
- Launching operations in New York with great success.

[Links] Web: getgrover.com Facebook: getgrover Twitter: @getgrover Instagram: getgrover

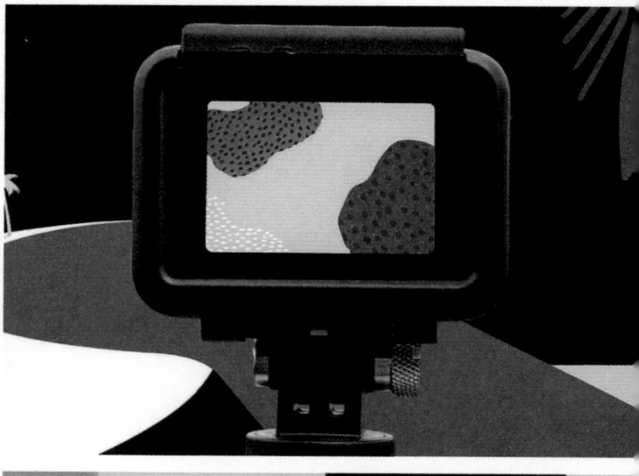

Rethink
things

[Name]

Infarm

[Elevator Pitch]

"We're pioneering farming as a service to provide urban communities with fresh, nutritious produce at affordable prices. By distributing our farms in the city, we cut the long supply chain, improving the quality and environmental footprint of our produce."

[The Story]

Erez Galonska, Guy Galonska and Osnat Michaeli founded Infarm in 2013 with the desire to grow their own food, live healthier, and become sustainable (and independent) without giving up their beloved city living. "We built the first pipe garden in our apartment living room," Osnat says, "and the outcome was mind-blowing. It was a cold, snowy February in Berlin, but inside we had a lush garden of yummy vegetables and greens. We wanted to bring the magic of growing plants to everybody and decided to start Infarm."

They decided to convert a 1955 Airstream trailer into a vertical farm, where plants would grow on shelves with LED lights glowing overhead. They parked their mobile farm in one of Berlin's most well-known urban farms, Prinzessinengarten. Aside from being a novel greenhouse, it served as an interactive installation. "Visitors could come and see a non-traditional way of farming, harvest herbs and microgreens, make bowls of salads, and plant new seeds for the next visitors." The trailer became both their research station and a lab where varied voices formed the beginnings of what today is called Infarm. In 2016, Infarm introduced the first in-store farm in the world in METRO Cash & Carry in Berlin followed by a second in-store-farm in Makro Antwerp. "We believe our food system should be decentralized," says Osnat, "and food production should get closer to the consumer."

[Funding History]

Bootstrap Seed Angel External

Infarm was awarded a €2 million grant plus undisclosed amounts from the European Commission as part of the H2020 program and European Pioneers. It closed a €4 million seed round led by Cherry Ventures followed by a Series A round of €20 million round led by Balderton Capital.

[Milestones]

- Founding the company in September 2013.
- Inventing and patenting a growing tray that allows fresh produce to be harvested daily at a significantly higher output than comparable technologies.
- Getting awarded a grant from the European Commission as part of the H2020 program.
- Introducing the world's first in-store farm in METRO Cash & Carry in Berlin.

[Links] Web: infarm.com Facebook: infarm.de Instagram: infarm

infarm

infarm

[Name]

Jaspr Trades

[Elevator Pitch]

"We've created a digital platform that lets people trade their talents and unneeded valuables, cash-free, with the people around them."

[The Story]

Jaspr is old-school bartering with modern technology, and it all started as a computer science thesis project for founder Noel Wigdor back in his native Canada. "In my late teens, I was obsessed with the fact that there are plenty of ways to buy and sell online, and yet no one had taken on trading successfully and made it easy to find someone that has something you want and also wants something you have." As part of the thesis, a basic version of Jaspr was used on Noel's campus, and he saw a diverse array of trading take place, including books being traded for car rides to the ski slope. Noel eventually found himself in Berlin and joined up with Vitalii Zurian and Steve Duncan to bring trading into the twenty-first century. They built the first prototype and tested it with one thousand participants, and the results spurred them to get serious.

Jaspr is a website and an app where people offer up and exchange items and services, and on any given day people may be offering art classes, plants, bikes, ride-sharing or even fake Facebook likes. For Noel, being able to offer a place for people to find treasures, offload items, or swap services hasn't been the only gratifying aspect. "Trading often means sharing your time and unique talents with others, and this often results in meaningful connections being made."

[Funding History]

Jaspr was a fortunate recipient of an EXIST Business Start-up Grant for €135,000 in 2016. This was followed by a successful Kickstarter campaign that pulled in €10,000. It has also received additional funding from two undisclosed angel investors.

[Milestones]

- **Founding the company in September of 2016.**
- **Going into public beta in December 2016.**
- **Raising €10,000 in our 2017 Kickstarter campaign.**
- **Launching our service on Android and IOS in March of 2017.**

[Links] Web: **jasprtrades.com** Facebook: **jasprtrades** Twitter: **@JasprTrades** Instagram: **jasprtrades**

SKIP

1.27
1.28
1.29
1.30
1.31
1.32

[Name]

Kontist

[Elevator Pitch]

"We're a banking solution designed exclusively for the self-employed. We empower independent workers with a fresh take on business banking in Germany."

[The Story]

Kontist was founded in 2016 by Christopher Plantener as a result of his frustration with the traditional banks and their failure to recognize the freelance and self-employed community as a market or to provide financial tools and services to meet their specific needs. He's since been joined by cofounders Madison Bell, Alexander Baatz and Sebastian Galonska, and together they have created a banking service that enables freelancers to stay on top of their finances with minimal hassle. Christopher and his cohorts believe that the number of self-employed is rising. "We believe this is the start of a revolution that will change how we work and live, allowing us to be more flexible and follow our passion."

Kontist wants to make money management as easy for the self-employed as it is for full-time employees. To this end, it has created a banking service that allows the user to open a business bank account from their phones, order a Mastercard, monitor cash flow, categorize expenses and reconcile bank statements with accounting records, all in the same app. Kontist accomplished this by integrating accounting solutions into its own digital platform through partnerships with accounting-software providers. Using its insights into business activity, Kontist's own in-built tax engine calculates income and sales-tax liabilities and stores them in virtual sub-accounts, so the user only sees their disposable net income in the account balance.

[Funding History]

External

Christopher Plantener's business idea of a banking solution tailored to the needs of freelancers piqued the interest of Danish company builder Founders. Thus far, Founders has provided Kontist with early-stage capital of €5 million.

[Milestones]

- Launching our service in 2017 with the iPhone app, followed by the Android app.
- Launching our own Business Debit Mastercard in September 2017, after having to overcome a number of bureaucratic barriers.
- Generating the first revenues from Mastercard fees and interchange.
- Securing our financing round.

[Links] Web: kontist.com Facebook: kontistHQ Twitter: @Kontist

6,429.50 €
3,730€
0€
Margarete-Restaurant
Margarete-Restaurant
Future Airlines
Reiserucksack GmbH
6,429.50 €
Kontist

prog

rams

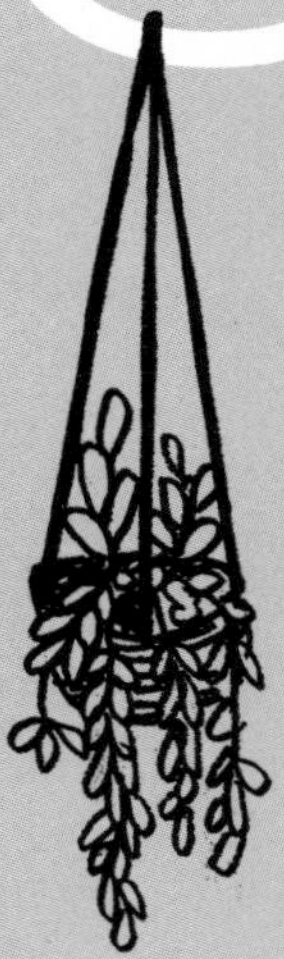

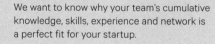

- **Have a strong team.**
  We want to know why your team's cumulative knowledge, skills, experience and network is a perfect fit for your startup.

- **Think about whether your startup is scalable.**
  Your business ideas should be in the pre-seed or seed stage but also scalable. So think about whether your idea or startup is a scalable venture case.

- **Have a product roadmap.**
  Where are you currently on the product roadmap? What is your long-term vision? You should be able to answers these questions when thinking about your startup's strategy.

- **Consider the timing.**
  Like the saying goes, timing is everything. We want to know why your startup is relevant and why the timing is right, right now.

[Name]

APX Axel Springer Porsche

[Elevator Pitch]

"We support excellent teams with scalable ideas to become successful venture companies. We offer investment, individual mentoring, and networking support in order to facilitate funding and cooperation opportunities. We invest at pre-seed and seed-stage."

[Sector]

Digital Business Models

[Description]

APX is a joint venture by Axel Springer and Porsche. Though the two companies may look different at first glance, both are well-known brands that value great customer experiences and innovative technology. The team of APX also built Axel Springer Plug and Play (ASPnP), which has invested in 102 companies. Thanks to open-minded owners and investors who are committed to a cross-industry focus, APX runs a rolling program to help pre-seed and seed startups become investor-ready. They accept new startups every month, with no application deadline. Additionally, APX's pre-seed deal is €25,000 for 5 percent equity. Their seed deal is up to €100,000 on a convertible basis if entrepreneurs have already raised external seed capital, and the equity is then negotiated on a case-by-case basis. Admitted teams have the freedom to pursue the areas they see as most important. Taking the long view, APX invests in teams with "digital user-centric business models" and provides them with solid foundations to take their next critical steps.

Thanks to shareholders' participation in this process, new startups can count on a substantive value discussion from the start. The process of getting into the program is quite selective, but once accepted, resources are generous. These come in the form of not only capital, expertise and networks but also access to engineers familiar with a Porsche standard of excellence. While at the APX space on Markgrafenstraße, startups work with venture developers and coaches to build their businesses and transform their ideas into valuable, data-driven products with traction and momentum. Other opportunities exist as well, and APX continues to invest in the companies if and when external investors become involved. The joint venture is also first-rate in their contract creation. The personalized, carefully-crafted investment contracts ensure solid communication between entrepreneurs and APX, which reassures a startup that it has the freedom and the resources to pursue their ideas to the fullest extent.

[Apply to]

hello@apx.ac

[Links]

Web: **apx.ac** Twitter: **@joinAPX** Facebook: **apxac** Instagram: **@joinAPX**

- **Have a clear focus.**
  It's not feasible to be good at everything, so pivot to what you're best at and excel at that. Focus, focus, focus.

- **Show your traction.**
  Know your potential marketplace and have proven traction with customers.

- **Stay in stealth mode.**
  Have a clear strategy so that once you communicate with the outside world, it's to enhance business, as opposed to cleaning up after PR released too soon.

- **Solve a real problem.**
  Look to solve issues or problems in the real world that relate to what people want to pay for and what investors would spend their money on. You can't solve everything, so focus on one issue or problem to gain trust.

[Name]

Beyond1435

[Elevator Pitch] *"We're an innovation platform where corporations and startups come together to make meaningful and impactful business in the fields of mobility and logistics."*

[Sector] **Mobility, logistics**

[Description] Now in its second year of operation, Beyond1435 is an open platform for startups seeking joint business-development projects and potential investments. The platform unites startups with companies such as Deutsche Bahn, Siemens, Bombardier Transportation and the Swiss Federal Railways. This friendly "one-stop shop" for startups is "a platform in which you meet decision-makers on the corporate and investor side, get to pitch your ideas, and try to implement long-lasting and robust business relationships with those corporations," says Deutsche Bahn's Marius Pigulla. A neutral operator, taking on an advisory role, helps support the platform at an operational level and builds international business partnerships with VCs, scouting agencies, innovation hubs and globally leading corporations. Startups accepted into the platform are paired with two or more corporate partners, and both startups and corporates come together for three-day Nexus meetings in Berlin. At these meetings, startups get the opportunity to pitch to corporates and have one-on-one sessions "to find points of overlap in order to work jointly together."

Beyond1435 is an initiative that grew out of an accelerator approach at Deutsche Bahn. This was combined with four years of looking at the best practices of corporate innovation. The platform comprises people who have run accelerator and incubator programs, come from venture capital and marketing backgrounds, and have founded startups themselves. "What's unique to this platform is that we have experience in all those fields, and we also know the downsides," says Marius. "We're trying to get the best out of all those worlds and combine them into this platform." Beyond1435 seeks to work with corporate-ready startups with existing traction (Series A+). "We want to see the traction of these startups, and if we see that and we can help with joint business development, we're also able to get them finance from strategic investors."

[Apply to] **beyond1435.com**

[Links] Web: **beyond1435.com** Facebook: **Beyond1435** Twitter: **@Beyond1435**

- **Be innovative and have growth potential.**
  One key target of enpact is job creation. Therefore, we support you in helping your economy to create jobs. If this is done in an innovative way, even better.

- **Have the personality of a founder.**
  We're interested in what drives you, and you need to be ready to share and learn both vertically and horizontally.

- **Be ready to make a social impact.**
  We consider our participants as drivers of change – economically, socially and personally. We look for future role models.

- **Be committed to networking and life-long learning.**
  We also look for people who are multipliers and stay engaged by becoming mentors and multipliers themselves.

[Name] **enpact**

[Elevator Pitch] *"We're a nonprofit organization that fosters the development of relationships and exchange among young entrepreneurs from geographically diverse startup ecosystems. We combine entrepreneurship and development work with innovative programs such as mentoring, space-creation, urban ecosystem evaluation and education."*

[Sector] **International development, education**

[Description] enpact was established with the aim of uniting entrepreneurs, strengthening economic relations between Europe and developing nations, and supporting the development of local economies with a big focus on the African and Middle Eastern regions. This goal was realized with five different projects: Startup Meter (a tool for gauging local startup ecosystems and how they might benefit from outside involvement); Startup Connect (founder delegations to different startup scenes worldwide); Mentoring Toolbox (for those wanting to design their own mentoring programs); Startup Space (coworking spaces in Berlin, Tunisia and Egypt, with more planned); and Startup Mentoring (the primary focus of what enpact does).

For Startup Mentoring, enpact has implemented programs that combine participants from Europe with those from either the West Africa or East Africa program, both of which are also open for Tunisian-based startups. Each program takes in ten startups from Europe and twenty startups from the host region. Localized Startup Mentoring programs are also offered in Tunisia, Ghana and Kenya. The eight-month-long programs kick off with preparatory workshops for startups and mentors, who will then maintain regular contact throughout the programs to track the startup's progress. They also include two five-day startup camps that offer intensive workshops (for example, on subjects such as pitching and honing the MVP) and network sessions with members of the local startup scene. These are a great opportunity for participants to meet expert founders and fellow entrepreneurs and make lasting connections and friendships.

Upon completion of the program, all participants become part of enpact's alumni network, which provides access to monthly events and startup safaris and to a vast network of B2B and B2C entrepreneurs. With additional training, alumni can themselves become mentors in future programs, thereby sharing their knowledge and enhancing their own mentoring experiences.

[Apply to] **enpact.org**

[Links] Website: **enpact.org** Facebook: **enpact** Twitter: **@enpact_startup**

- **A stable and solid founding team.**
  We're looking for balanced and cohesive teams capable of delivering results.

- **Market-ready, mature product or service.**
  The product should have been battle-tested with a few customers already. We want to help you build a better business, not just help you sell your product within METRO. We'll leverage the Techstars and METRO networks to help you achieve your goals.

- **A product that can be tested and used in Europe.**
  Make sure your team (and product) is capable of deploying into Europe. We'll help you through the process, but you must be physically and emotionally ready.

- **Have glowing customer reviews.**
  Get your first or earliest customers to be your champions; those are the best referrals!

[Name]

METRO Accelerator

[Elevator Pitch] *"We're a highly selective mentorship program for technology-first startups across the entire value chain of hospitality and retail."*

[Sector] **B2B enterprise, hospitality, retail**

[Description] METRO Accelerator (powered by Techstars) specializes in the hospitality and retail industries, offering two three-month programs per year, with ten startups selected for each. In the Retail Program, startups can test their solutions across the METRO and P&G supply chains while building business networks and receiving individualized help and support. The program is strategically integrated with unparalleled access to the intellectual capital of METRO, one of the world's most extensive wholesale and food networks. The Hospitality Program is an accelerator that focuses on tech startups with restaurants or hotels as customers. It gives startups the opportunity to test their product in over five hundred restaurants and hotels.

In many accelerator environments, startups receive nurturing and support but may still lack the ability to deal with potential large enterprise clients. Both programs place a large emphasis on ensuring startups are ready to run pilots with large corporates like METRO and P&G. In addition, both programs are open internationally, and the accelerator team travels Europe and Asia to recruit companies with diverse ideas that are ready for the European market. Startups will receive investment funding between €20,000 and €120,000 for 6 to 10 percent equity; more than $2 million worth of perks from over one hundred companies such as AWS, Google, Sendgrid, Silicon Valley Bank and other partners; intense, hands-on mentorship from Techstars & METRO experts, giving them proven methods for business development, customer acquisition and recruitment; and lifetime connections to the Techstars global network of founders, investors, alumni, partners and mentors. Top METRO and P&G decision-makers attend the programs not only to give startups unique insights into working with some of the world's largest companies but also to commit to proof-of-concepts and plan commercial deals.

[Apply to] **metroaccelerator.com**

[Links] Web: **metroaccelerator.com** Facebook: **metroaccel** Twitter: **@ METROAccel** Instagram: **metroaccel**

- **You are a serial entrepreneur, enthusiastic technologist or industry expert.**
  You've founded a startup before, have working knowledge of technology, or specialize in a particular industry.

- **Are ready to dive into future technologies.**
  You're excited about IoT, blockchain or distributed systems.

- **Have a pitch deck prepared to convey your idea to us.**
  You've got a method to express your idea, have done some initial research, and have an 'ideal' industry partner in mind.

- **Think BIG but know how to break down tasks in an agile way.**
  You dream up solutions to real-world problems and are open to learning from experts about best practices in business modeling.

- **Play well with others.**
  You're motivated to work with NBT's diverse, interdisciplinary team and venture community.

[Name]

Next Big Thing

[Elevator Pitch]

"We're a Berlin-based company builder offering agile and effective acceleration of Internet of Things and blockchain ventures. Through business mentorship, technology expertise and funding, we launch startups that promote digital transformation and IoT-driven innovation in Europe."

[Sector] **IoT, blockchain**

[Description]

Next Big Thing (NBT), a company builder that combines incubator and accelerator with operational VC, connects entrepreneurs with corporate partners and provides technological and business-modeling expertise. NBT nurtures entrepreneurs and early-stage startups through a lean venture-development process, sharing both risks and successes. NBT has successfully launched numerous ventures across industries while developing its own tech stack in blockchain and secure hardware.

Entrepreneurs get a head start via in-house engineering support and hardware-development experience as they work towards their proof of concept – all with the aim of convincing NBT that the idea is worth building into a company. The next step is building a demonstrator to convince a partner, often an industry partner with domain knowledge, followed by an MVP. The entire process is supported by the core NBT Team and the NBT Engineering Team, and includes access to an IoT-hardware lab. Ventures receive pre-seed funding and matched industry-partner funding and gain entry to Berlin's vital startup ecosystem. NBT's own ecosystem consists of investors, startups, corporate partners, hardware and software engineers, and technology providers. Ventures interact in a collaborative setting that encourages parallel learning.

Through corporate partnerships, NBT builds relationships with key industry players ready to innovate and get to market faster. The newly formed companies have startup agility, market research and corporate resources. By building great companies, NBT promotes digital transformation and IoT-driven innovation for SMEs. A partnership between NBT, Factory Berlin and Fraunhofer Institute now forms the de:hub for IoT, a Germany-wide digital innovation initiative. NBT invites entrepreneurs at the concept stage to discuss how to utilize IoT or blockchain for new business models. Entrepreneurs, technologists and interested corporate partners are encouraged to join the community via social channels and attend NBT events, workshops, meetups and hackathons across Europe.

[Apply to] **hub.nextbigthing.ag/entrepreneur-application**

[Links] Web: **nextbigthing.ag** Facebook: **NextBigThing.AG** Twitter: **@nbt_ag**

- **Be a post-seed startup.**
  We're looking for startups that either just completed their seed round or are looking for Series A funding.

- **Be Business-to-Business.**
  Having a B2B transaction model isn't a requirement, but it is one of our priorities.

- **Have a minimum viable product that works.**
  This one is firm. You need to have a functioning product ready to sell or develop with our network of top-tier corporations and investors.

- **Have the capacity for multiple pilot projects.**
  This can mean you've already got a team of full-time employees that can handle multiple accounts or you have a technology that's incredibly easy to scale.

- **Come to the table with at least one corporate client.**
  Having a track record of happy customers is a big plus, but not mandatory.

- **Specialize in smart mobility, supply chain, energy or circular economies.**
  Having product applications in these areas will up your chances of getting accepted.

[Name]

Plug and Play Berlin

[Elevator Pitch] *"We're a global startup ecosystem and Silicon Valley's most active VC specializing in the development of early-to-growth stage startups. We provide a global platform through established programs in Europe, the Americas, and Asia."*

[Sector] **Energy, greentech, mobility, logistics**

[Description] Plug and Play is a place for innovators to connect with cutting-edge technologies and where corporations, startups and venture capitalists meet within a single ecosystem to shape sustainable digital transformations. Through tailored deal flow, themed workshops and face-to-face interaction, the platform enables corporations to engage with startups that can either complement their core business or help create new revenue streams. Most importantly, startups gain access to different business units of the largest multinational companies.

Germany is both a global role model for green energy and a home to industry-leading logistics companies, and since Berlin is a major hub within Europe's startup ecosystem, it was the obvious place for the VC giant from Silicon Valley to base its new endeavors. Starting in 2013, Plug and Play worked behind the scenes to launch two of Berlin's most noteworthy startup incubators: the Axel Springer Plug and Play Accelerator and Beyond1435. It now operates STARTUP AUTOBAHN, a Stuttgart-based innovation platform connecting some of the best mobility startups with Germany's legendary automotive sector. Recently, it also launched two new verticals of its own in Berlin: Energy & Sustainability and Supply Chain & Logistics. On top of all that, it plans to launch a handful of additional programs here by the end of 2019.

Plug and Play accepts applications on a rolling basis and is always looking for innovative startups to be part of its global network. As part of both recently launched programs, Plug and Play brings stakeholders to Berlin for networking and innovation round tables called Focus Weeks. During each Focus Week, promising startups meet one-on-one with Plug and Play's corporate partners. This personalized deal flow makes up the core of the platform and acts as a stage gate for the next official batch of pilot projects. Plug and Play also organizes public community meetups that are open to entrepreneurs, investors, university students and anyone else with a passion for innovation.

[Apply to] **Energy & Sustainability: Brittany Salas / brittany@pnptc.com**
Supply Chain & Logistics: Max Philp / max@pnptc.com

[Links] Web: **pnptc.com** Facebook: **Plug-and-Play-Europe** Twitter: **@pnpeurope**

- **Be an expert.**
  We're looking for early-stage startups that are experts in the particular domain they're working in.

- **Have an enterprise or technology product.**
  It's crucial to have a product that is an innovative enterprise solution, leverages artificial intelligence or uses machine learning.

- **Have a strong team with the ability to make your idea a reality.**
  It's important that your team has the skills, ambition, strong technical capabilities and motivation to pull off your idea. Not only that, we hope that your team believes that leveraging SAP data, APIs or platform technologies will deliver additional value to our customers.

- **Be motivated.**
  If you and your team are driven to expand your network, develop your product, accelerate your company's growth and gain a stronger foothold in Berlin and Germany, we want to hear from you.

[Name]

SAP.iO Foundry Berlin

[Elevator Pitch]

"We're among the first dedicated enterprise-solution and machine-learning accelerators in Europe. Our mission is to grow a generation of revolutionary software businesses in the SAP ecosystem. The European flagship SAP.iO Foundry in Berlin focuses on machine learning and AI."

[Sector]

Social Entrepreneurship, Inclusive Entrepreneurship and Intrapreneurship

[Description]

Specializing in the creation of state-of-the-art software, the SAP.iO program is designed to provide early-stage startups with expert strategic and financial guidance; namely, how to understand their value to customers and zero in on it. Startups are also given access to SAP technology, data and APIs and have the opportunity to refine their products through numerous user interactions with SAP's 350,000+ customers across nearly every enterprise vertical. This is achieved through a combination of workshops and special training from both within and outside of SAP. The primary aim of its accelerator programs is to identify new innovative use cases and business opportunities as well as to expand SAP's ecosystem with new business and technology solutions that have the potential to revolutionize entire industries.

A mentor-driven approach to helping entrepreneurs is an important part of what makes the SAP.iO Foundry stand out. Currently, it provides startups with cutting-edge feedback regarding how they assemble solutions, construct their business models, acquire funding, and adopt a concise go-to-market strategy. In addition to functional assistance and investments, the SAP.iO programs provide startup teams with support and guidance on how to best tailor their sales and marketing approach to reach their full growth potential.

SAP's long-standing reputation of being an open driver of innovation and collaboration is another part of what makes SAP.iO a highly effective partner for startups. With an eye for innovative solutions and a commitment to bringing the very best emerging technologies to SAP customers, the Berlin Foundry runs two accelerator programs focusing on enterprise solutions and on leveraging machine learning across all sectors. Thanks to an effective combination of tech-centric training and support, startups receive invaluable insights into a range of topics, including product development, industry specifications, SaaS and B2B business development, and B2B sales.

[Apply to]

https://www.f6s.com/sap.iofoundryberlin

[Links]

Web: **sap.io/foundry** Facebook: **SAP.iOFoundry** Twitter: **@sap_iO** Instagram: **SAPiOBerlinFoundry**

- **Be working on industrial solutions for IoT.**
  Since the program entails working closely with SAP development product units in the realms of Industry 4.0, manufacturing, digital supply chain and asset management, it's important that your startup is working on industrial solutions for IoT.

- **Have solutions that are complementary to SAP's offerings.**
  This element is crucial because we assess the unique needs of each individual startup and identify key co-innovation opportunities to see how it can grow alongside the SAP product portfolio.

- **Have products and prototypes.**
  Your startup should be at a stage where you already have a product or a minimum viable product when applying.

- **Have more than one cofounder.**
  Your startup team should have at least two cofounders.

[Name]

SAP IoT Startup Accelerator

[Elevator Pitch]

"We're a globally accessible co-innovation program for selected B2B startups innovating in the world of Industry 4.0, manufacturing, digital supply chain, and asset management."

[Sector]

IoT, manufacturing, digital supply chain, asset management

[Description]

Few companies have a stronger support system for industrial startups than SAP. As the IoT industry continues to change, SAP is prepared to keep growing and evolving with it. With a specialty for giving B2B startups the momentum they need, SAP assesses the unique needs of each individual startup and identifies key " co-innovation opportunities," where the startup can grow alongside the SAP product portfolio. This includes plotting a path to exactly what success looks like for each individual startup. Throughout this process of co-innovation, SAP assists teams by exposing them to their sizable customer base. The startups work closely together with the SAP development product units in the areas of Industry 4.0, manufacturing, digital supply chain and asset management. "It was, and still is, one of the best experiences we had with a global company," says Loginno cofounder Shachar Tal. "With the IoT Accelerator team's close support, we were able to produce our dream product, built on top of the logistics industry's number-one platform."

The SAP IoT Startup Accelerator offers selected startups centrally located office space in Berlin. In addition to strong connections within Berlin's ever-expanding startup scene, the accelerator is also just a few hours from SAP's headquarters in Walldorf, Germany, and directly connected to the SAP Labs Berlin and Potsdam innovation network, making contact with corporates fairly common. SAP's network also reaches outside of Germany. The program is strongly connected to SAP Silicon Valley with parts of the team supporting startups out of Palo Alto. Both locations are aligning the best tech, talent and timing to make valuable, lasting change to the IoT industry at large. "What I can honestly say is that SAP runs one of the best – if not the best – IoT startup program." says XMPro CEO Pieter van Schalkwyk. "Compared to other programs, they definitely move quicker and have a much more practical approach."

[Apply to]

https://www.f6s.com/sapiotstartupaccelerator/about

[Links]

Web: **sap.com/iot-startup** Twitter: **@IoT_Accelerator**

- **Have a strong and skilled team.**
  We look for three characteristics in your team: complementary skills, experience and commitment.

- **Have a compelling idea.**
  We want our startups to solve real problems in a unique and optimal way.

- **Should already have traction.**
  Our startups focus on their key metrics and accomplish them quickly.

- **Identify your market.**
  Our startups should target exciting, disruptive and growing markets.

[Name]

Techstars Berlin

[Elevator Pitch] *"We're the worldwide network that helps entrepreneurs succeed."*

[Sector] **All verticals**

[Description]

Techstars is a worldwide network with over forty mentorship-driven accelerator programs in many cities across the globe. The Techstars Berlin Accelerator, like its international counterparts, is a highly selective three-month-long accelerator that usually invests in ten startups each year. Being a mentorship-driven program, it draws from a large pool of mentors committed to helping startups accelerate their businesses. Mentors include entrepreneurs, experts, and investors from leading VCs. Startups are introduced to dozens of mentors in the first few weeks and keep working closely with up to five of them afterwards.

Techstars also has the support of skilled associates to help startups focus on functional business areas such as fundraising, digital marketing, tech, business development and operations, among others. These skilled associates work closely with the startups during the program and, in many cases, afterwards too. This allows startups to get to know potential key employees for a considerable time before deciding whether or not to incorporate them into the team. Techstars supports each of their startups with over $1 million worth of perks from global network partners such as AWS, Google for Entrepreneurs, SendGrid, Cooley, Dentons, and other high-profile tech players.

The program concludes with a Demo Day for startups to present their business to investors and to the wider entrepreneurial community. However, Techstars support doesn't stop there. It supports its startups on a continuing basis with advice, connections and exclusive events like Techstars BizDev Days, Techstars Investor Days, and Techstars FounderCon, as well as through ongoing mentorship, monthly alumni events and access to a deep well of resources.

One of the unique features of any Techstars Accelerator program is the equity-back guarantee, which ensures that founders get the best possible experience and development of their business. This key characteristic goes to show the confidence that Techstars has in its accelerators and the high-quality standards it demands of itself, as well as of its investments.

[Apply to] **techstars.com/apply**

[Links] Web: **techstars.com/programs/berlin-program** Facebook: **techstars** Twitter: **@techstars**

- **A vision for creating smarter urban areas.**
  We want to work with startups that are committed to making urban areas smarter, greener and more resource-efficient.

- **Have a novel and innovative approach to global problems.**
  We're thrilled to see new and different ways of addressing the problems that matter most, especially with new technologies or integrated solutions.

- **Be a good strategic fit to Wilo's core business.**
  We're looking for young enterprises who work at the intersection of smart building and water innovation.

- **Have already established a unique fit in the market and be looking to scale.**
  Startups should be past their seed stage of growth and be ready for Series A investment.

- **Have strong relationships with other investors.**
  We're keen to see startups with a diverse funding strategy and the secured support of other investors.

[Name]

Wincubator

[Elevator Pitch]

"We create smarter and more sustainable urban areas through innovation and investment."

[Sector]

Cleantech, digitalization

[Description]

Wilo is one of the world's leading manufacturers of pumps and pump systems for the building, water and industrial sectors. Wilo launched the Wincubator as their innovation and investment arm to initiate new clean and sustainable solutions. The Wincubator, through investment or cocreation, supports startups addressing challenges related to climate change and rapid urbanization, such as water scarcity or energy shortages. Wincubator organizers are particularly interested in working with startups that are developing solutions around water or construction technology.

For investment cases, they're looking for startups fundraising for Series A funds (big bonus if they've already secured other investors). The Wincubator wants to see that a startup already has a strong track record, a solid customer base and at least €100,000 per year in sales. Additionally, it prefers startups backed up by a diverse and focused management team with nice chemistry between the founders or core team. The Wincubator's ticket size is around €500,000 to €1 million; however, they always handle a startup's financial needs on a case-by-case basis.

For cocreation cases, the Wincubator stands strong on the belief that the best way to innovate is to collaborate. This is why they welcome new enterprises interested in taking their businesses to the next level. Depending on what the startup wants to do, the Wincubator can tap its global network of industry professionals, coinvestors and other expert partners in the water-management sector to help actualize ideas and build something amazing together. First the startup approaches the Wincubator with an idea, which will be evaluated on how it can complement Wilo and in which area it can receive support. Together, through in-person meetings, the Wincubator and the startup create a project proposal for Wilo. Within Wilo, the right business unit and people are introduced to the startup. If approved, the proposal will then be transformed into a living, breathing, jointly implemented project.

[Apply to]

wincubator.com/contact

[Links]

Web: **wincubator.com**

spa

ces

[Name]
Ahoy! Berlin

[Address] Wattstraße 11, 13355 Berlin

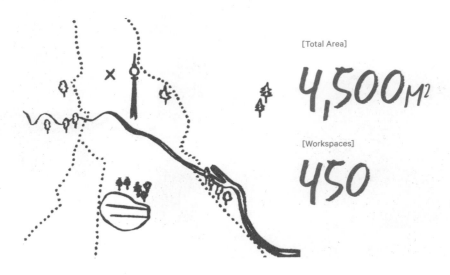

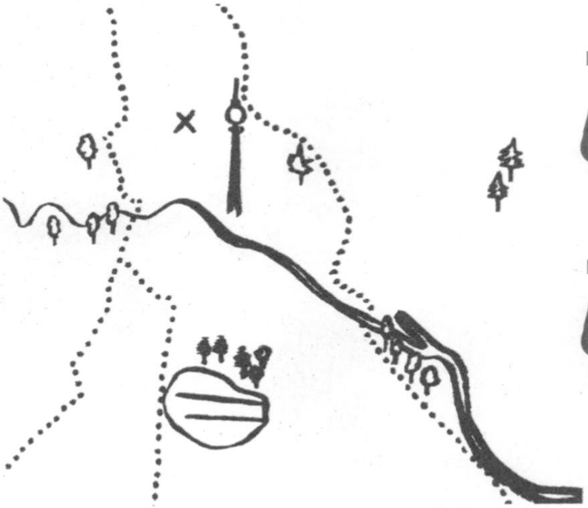

[Total Area]

4,500 m²

[Workspaces]

450

[The Story]

Founded in 2012 by Nikita Roshkow and Nikolas Woischnik, Ahoy! Berlin is located on the edge of the Wedding district in an imposing 1950s former factory building. The nautical name represents a stable ship to jump onto and sail the stormy seas of innovation and entrepreneurship. As the first tech organization in the neighborhood, Ahoy! Berlin stimulated the regeneration of the surrounding area and created a new local tech-focused ecosystem. Ahoy! is a space for coworking and innovation, where individuals and companies work side by side in a playful and cozy environment.

The careful design of the vast space provides the warmest of welcomes, with the generous common area downstairs for gatherings of up to one hundred fifty guests, two full-time chefs catering for the community, and the barista who serves freshly roasted coffee at the cafe. Ahoy! Berlin uses the building's lofty scale to full effect, with an interior crafted with personality, passion and creativity. Old doors and other reclaimed furniture have been converted into design elements, giving character to the whitened walls. Member desks are dotted around the different working spaces, which range over three floors. With five conference rooms bookable for non-members, even visitors can get a taste of the diversity and energy of the space, which is often running at almost full capacity.

[Links] Web: ahoyberlin.com Facebook: ahoyberlin Twitter: @ahoyberlin Instagram: ahoyberlin

Face of the Space:

Ahoy! Berlin cofounders Nikita Roshkow and Nikolas Woischnik met in 2012. After taking the opportunity to lease the vacant property, they soon started the coworking space. Nikita manages the day-to-day business operation, combining his business background with his passion to work with startups. Nikolas, who is also founder of Tech Open UG and Openers, focuses his energy on supporting the community, and the local emerging-tech startup ecosystem.

SOFT DRINKS
FRESH JUICES
Mix it up!
Orange
Apple
Beetroot
Carrot
Mint
Ginger
3,40
HOT DRINKS
FRESH TEAS:
Ginger
Mint
Lemon
2,40€
TEA
TEA TALES:
Forever Young Tea
Everything But Grey Earl
Up For English Breakfast
Good Morning Mate
Blueberry Cupcake
Matcha Tea
2,40€
Café Frappé
Iced Latte
Iced Coffee
ALCOHOL
Craft Beer Brlo 0,33l 4,00€
Red Wine 4,20€
Prosecco 3,00€
Gin Tonic 6,00€
Moscow Mule
Cuba Libre
Vodka Mate

[Name]

betahaus Berlin

[Address] Prinzessinnenstraße 19–20, 10969 Berlin

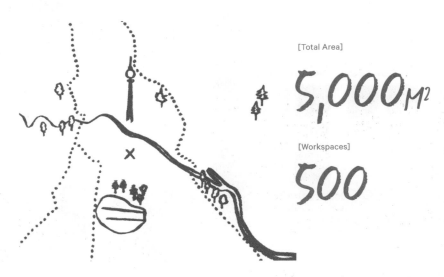

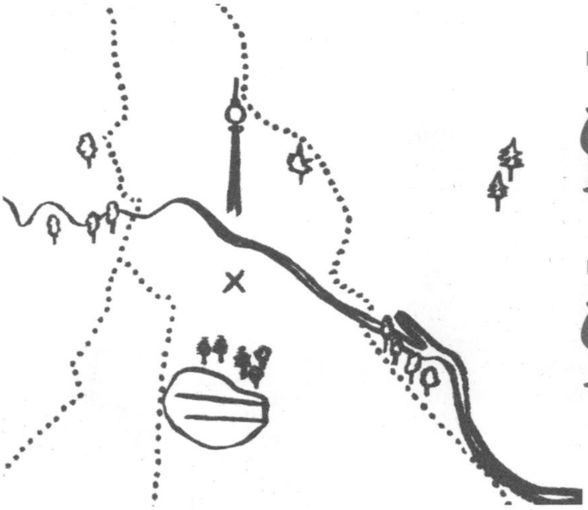

[Total Area]

5,000 M²

[Workspaces]

500

[The Story] When Christoph Fahle and his friends first decided they wanted to create a workshop space with a cool coffee shop where people could work on projects and fix bikes (among other things), they had no idea what to do – aside from setting out to acquire a large building. "The betahaus Berlin space was established at a time that 'startup' and 'coworking' weren't the buzzwords they are now," says Christoph, "so there was quite a bit of trial and error in getting our space right." They established the betahaus coworking space and community in a huge five-story building, and since then it has become an institution in the Berlin startup ecosphere. Nowadays, there are also a number of betahaus partner spaces elsewhere in Europe such as Hamburg, Sofia and Barcelona.

Soon betahaus will be relocated to even bigger premises, and just as they have in the past, Christoph and team are getting their members involved in the interior-design process. "We want an even cooler coffee shop, more event spaces, and team rooms with glass walls to keep up to date with the open and inviting nature of coworking spaces these days," he says. The new space will also include a rooftop garden terrace and even a small cold pool for taking a refreshing break from work.

[Links] Web: betahaus.com Facebook: betahaus Twitter: @betahaus Instagram: betahaus

Face of the Space:
Cofounder Christoph Fahle takes care of new ideas and projects at betahaus. When he's not doing that, he likes to geek around with electronics, travel and work on spin-off projects. Needless to say, he's always busy.

PRFCT

[Name]

Fab Lab Berlin

[Address] Prenzlauer Allee, 242, 10405 Berlin

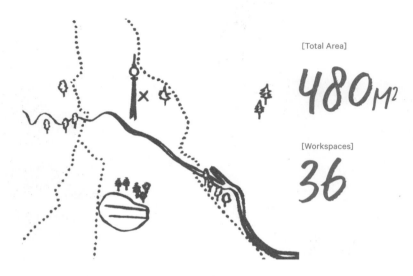

[Total Area]

480 M²

[Workspaces]

36

[The Story]

Fab Lab was originally an initiative of MIT (Massachusetts Institute of Technology) to give local community members access to the latest digital prototyping tools in an open digital fabrication studio. Fab Lab Berlin is but one of a global network of over one thousand Fab Labs (with more being opened on a regular basis) and it's located in what was a former brewery in the Prenzlauer Berg district of Berlin. Managing Director Daniel Heltzel says, "We provide a platform for students, freelance designers and engineers, and even corporates to team up for hardware prototyping and product development. We see a lot of exploration of new applications here and less actual production, as most of the final products are manufactured somewhere else. Places like Fab Lab Berlin are particularly valuable for teams working on first iterations of their prototypes."

Members can get training for rapid prototyping in one of the many workshops that happen through the year, and there are always others working on their own things nearby who will lend a helping hand. The space is outfitted with 3D printers, laser cutters, CNC routers, design software and electronics to help turn members' ideas into reality. Fab Lab also has a curated space where hardware startups, design agencies and research project groups reside.

[Links] Web: fablab.berlin Facebook: FabLabBerlin Twitter: @FabLabBLN Instagram: fablabberlin

Face of the Space:
Daniel Heltzel is Fab Lab Berlin's Managing Director and he is a trained social scientist who previously worked at the Indian Institute of Science and the University of Freiburg. "I love the dynamic nature of Fab Lab and seeing the projects come to life." he says.

[Name] # Factory Görlitzer Park

[Address] Lohmühlenstraße 65, 12435 Berlin

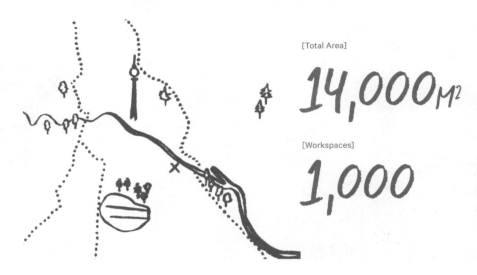

[Total Area]

14,000 M²

[Workspaces]

1,000

[The Story] Factory Görlitzer Park, covering a space of more than four football fields, sits next to the old rail line that connected to Görlitzer Bahnhof and passed through the former Berlin Wall area. It's the second campus under the Factory moniker (the first, Factory Mitte, opened in 2014). Factory started out primarily as a coworking space, but in 2016 it transformed into more of a business club model. Community manager Caleb Screpnek says that they wanted to differentiate it from other coworking spaces in Berlin. "Though there's a large variety of places to work, this isn't the kind of place where desktop computers are fixed in place. Rather than people working in one spot for the whole day, we want to inspire movement, where people can work for a couple of hours, get up and go to the cafe, then switch work places."

The building has seen diverse tenants throughout its years, beginning with a film chemical company and later hosting an assortment of small offices and freelancers. The massive five-floor building offers a vast array of workspaces and conference rooms as well as a restaurant, a café, a Hogwarts-style library, a meditation/yoga room and a movie theater with sofas. There's also the "playground," with ping-pong tables, lofts to climb into and escape, and even a ball pit for a leisurely paddle. "Creative spaces breed creativity," Caleb says.

[Links] Web: factoryberlin.com Facebook: FactoryBrln Twitter: @FactoryBerlin

Face of the Space:
Originally from Canada, Caleb Screpnek worked as an artist, producing and selling paintings. At Factory, his arts and business background mixed with his responsibilities for artist initiatives, and his role as community manager creates the perfect fusion.

for Entrepreneurs

[Name]

Google for Entrepreneurs

[Address] Lohmühlenstraße 65, 12435 Berlin

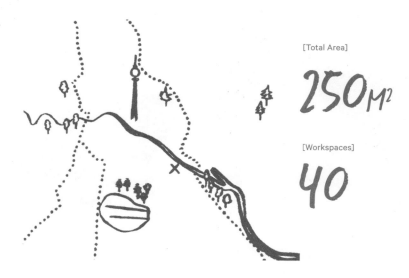

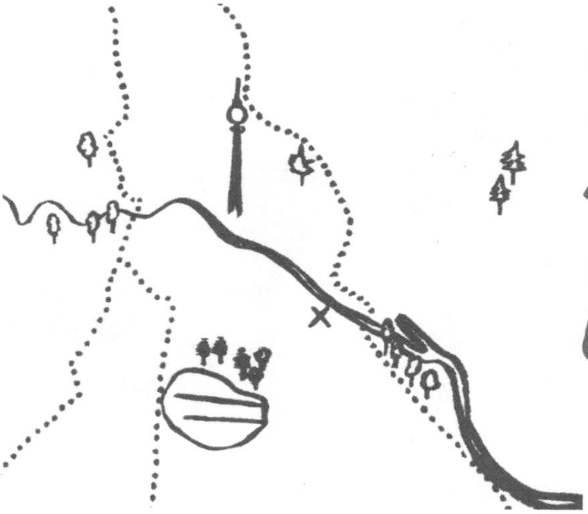

[Total Area]

250M²

[Workspaces]

40

[The Story]

Google for Entrepreneurs partners with startup communities and builds campuses where entrepreneurs can learn, connect and create companies with the potential to change the world. Since its founding, it has been actively supporting the Berlin startup ecosystem through its partner Factory and helping to build a strong community of entrepreneurs equipped with the skills and connections they need to realize their visions. The Google for Entrepreneurs hub inside Factory's Görlitzer Park building works to bring Google's resources to the broader startup community in Berlin.

With an event space for over one hundred people and a workshop space for forty, it regularly hosts "tech talks" from Google and community organizers, as well as hands-on workshops, one-on-one mentorship sessions and office hours. Along with direct access to Google experts, Factory members can also work from dozens of startup spaces in cities around the world using the Google for Entrepreneurs Passport. The Google for Entrepreneurs hub is only a five-minute bike ride from the Kreuzberg Umspannwerk, the future site of Campus Berlin. It will be Google's seventh campus and part of a global network open to anyone working on a big idea or already running a startup.

[Links] Web: **campus.co/berlin** Twitter: **@campus_berlin**

Face of the Space:
Rowan Barnett has been involved in the startup ecosystem as a founder, mentor and advisor since moving from London to Berlin in 2004. Now, as head of Google for Entrepreneurs Germany, he is passionate about using Google's resources to create a more inclusive ecosystem in Berlin and to help a new, diverse generation of entrepreneurs succeed. Previously, he drove digital media innovation at Axel Springer and led Twitter's growth across Europe.

Google
for Entrepreneurs

[Name]

KAOS Berlin

[Address] Wilhelminenhofstraße 92, 12459 Berlin

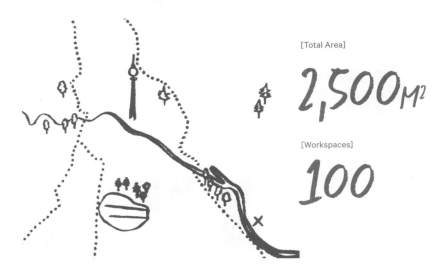

[Total Area]

2,500M²

[Workspaces]

100

[The Story]

The folks behind KAOS have transformed what was once the Transformationswerk and Kabelwerk factory on the banks of the river Spree into a bustling hive of activity. Cofounder Jascha Vogel and a collective of creatives from different disciplines came across the then-abandoned building after seeking a space for their own purposes. "The building was like a big kids' playground when we acquired it," Jascha says, "and we had fun refurbishing it for our own purposes." Once they'd turned it into a large, vibrant creative space, a number of others gravitated to KAOS as well, so it made sense to turn it into a publicly accessible coworking space.

KAOS is geared toward all creatives, and the huge space buzzes with artists and designers from all disciplines toiling away at their crafts. KAOS has a large main hall and comes equipped with rooms for woodworking, milling, metalworking and 3D printing. There's a desk space with eighteen fixed desks, but KAOS is meant to be more of an open and social space for collaborating and networking while working. KAOS also plays host to a range of events. "As the gentrification of the surrounding area took place," Jascha says, "we had to get creative with ways of keeping up with the rise in rent, so we have workshops, music shows, exhibitions and big art festivals."

[Links] Web: **kaosberlin.de** Facebook: **kaosberlin** Twitter: **@kaos_berlin** Instagram: **kaosberlin**

Face of the Space:
Jascha Vogel completed his studies as a media technology engineer before dabbling in two of his own startups. The need for a working space led him to KAOS and, subsequently, to his role as community manager. He says, "I fell into this organizing thing by way of no one else raising their hand."

[Name]

Mindspace

[Address] Skalitzer Straße 104, 10997 Berlin

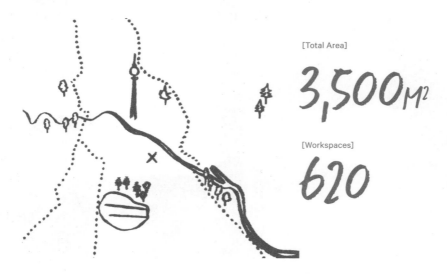

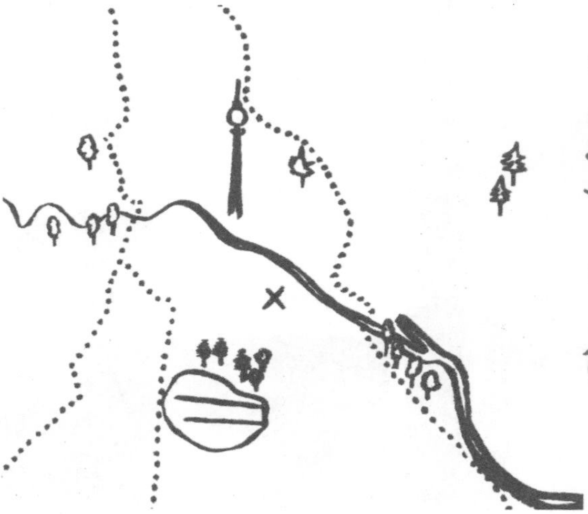

[Total Area]

3,500 M²

[Workspaces]

620

[The Story] Since Mindspace opened its first coworking space in Tel Aviv in 2014, it has been sprouting new locations at record speed, and today it has eighteen locations worldwide. One of the latest additions is on Skalitzer Straße, a main thoroughfare in the heart of Berlin's bustling Kreuzberg area and close to cafes, restaurants and several U-Bahn stations. Works by local artists adorn the walls, and an in-house design team has styled the interior to be as comfy as your home. The space is characterized by brick walls, wooden floors and high ceilings, and furnished with wall-to-wall bookshelves, colorful carpets and velour couches. Amenities include 24/7 access, a coffee bar and soda fountain, free utilities, and a well-stocked event space.

Members, who range from big teams to individual freelancers, can also make use of benefits – such as discounts on gym memberships, restaurants, cultural activities and business-related apps and services – offered by the partnerships between Mindspace and other companies. Mindspace places a special emphasis on fostering a strong community though frequent events, ranging from community breakfasts and themed happy hours to coding events and painting workshops.

[Links] Web: **mindspace.me** Facebook: **mindspace.me** Twitter: **@mindspaceME**

Face of the Space:

Edita Lobaciute was the first international employee Mindspace brought on board when they began their global expansion in 2015, and with her Lithuanian passport, Danish education and Polish-Russian roots, she's as global as the company. As Mindspace's Global Community Lead, she's in charge of organizing the community-driving strategies, and is especially focused on creating tailor-made events for Mindspace members.

EER

[Name] **Silicon Allee**

[Address] Chausseestraße 19, 10115 Berlin

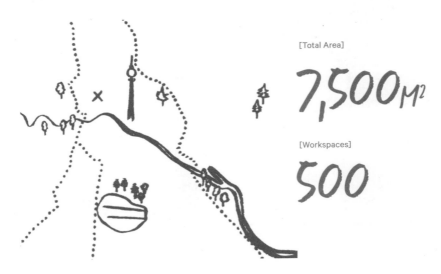

[Total Area]

7,500 m²

[Workspaces]

500

[The Story] Silicon Allee was started by entrepreneurs Travis Todd and Schuyler Deerman, whose time in San Francisco inspired them to build a startup community in Berlin with meetups, events and an English-language blog. Silicon Allee's first monthly meetup was hosted at Rosenthaler Platz in February 2011 and has been running ever since. Over the years, the term "Silicon Allee" has become synonymous with Berlin's tech ecosystem. Their mission has always been to connect Berlin's tech community with the rest of the world, and they act as a self-styled 'embassy,' helping locals gain international exposure and helping incoming internationals get connected locally.

On their fifth anniversary, Silicon Allee joined forces with Factory, an organization that develops and operates office spaces to create a working, living and event space for their vibrant startup community in Berlin. Their campus opened in 2017 with a stellar group of international and local technology companies in residence. The previously unremarkable '90s building proved a challenge to renovate, but they chose well, delivering a cool Japanese-minimalism-meets-tech look with contrasting bright, white offices and dark, cozy common areas. The early- and later-stage tech startups that populate the offices are given the flexibility to grow within the space. Silicon Allee continues to build out public and private spaces on campus, including several event venues, a summer beer-garden courtyard and a rooftop terrace.

[Links] Web: siliconallee.com Facebook: siliconallee Twitter: @siliconallee

Face of the Space:
Silicon Allee cofounder Travis Todd is an American national who has lived in Berlin for over eleven years. Travis, who has a background in design, coding and advertising, has founded four companies in Berlin but has been full time on Silicon Allee since 2015. When time permits, he loves surfing, Lisbon, beer and rock climbing.

HAUSWEIN WEISS
HAUSWEIN ROT
ICH KÜHLE MEINEN
MUT AN HANDARBEIT
COWORKING MEMBERSHIP
SELBSTBEDIENUNG - SELFSERVICE
ROTWEIN
SCHAUMWEIN
ZWICKEL
COFFEE NEVER SLEEPS
MEETING & WORKSHOP ROOMS
EVENT SPACES AVAILABLE

[Name]

St. Oberholz

[Address] Rosenthaler Straße 72a, 10119 Berlin

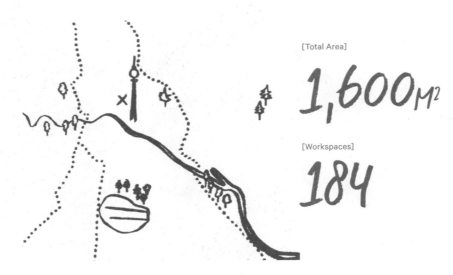

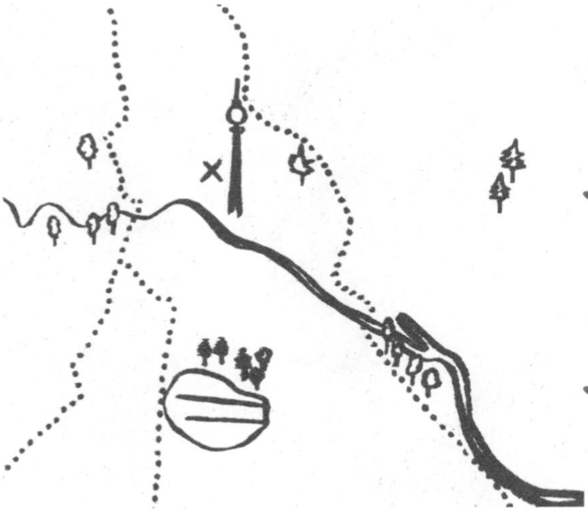

[Total Area]

1,600M2

[Workspaces]

184

[The Story]

Starting as a café in 2005, St. Oberholz is at least as old as the first coworking space in San Francisco and among the first to pioneer coworking in Germany. The tastefully retro interior, elegant ground-floor cafe and workspace-oriented upper floor at the Rosenthaler Platz location is a perfect union of pleasant atmosphere and efficient work environment. A standout space by today's standards, it was even more so ten years ago in a then much less startup-centric Berlin. St. Oberholz was among the first cafes in Germany to allow people to access wifi and charge their devices for free. According to coworking manager Tobias Kremkau, a critical feature that transformed the space from unique coffee shop into creative coworking space was the "very long tables." It was at these tables that digital nomads and entrepreneurs began discussing ideas and collaborating on new projects, which then grew into startups.

St. Oberholz has two Berlin spaces, both with a traditional café on the ground floor and workspaces above. The original space at Rosenthaler Platz has a more vintage DIY style and a charming spiral staircase, while the Zehdenicker Straße location has a more modern interior and a lift. Currently, St. Oberholz is taking what it learns from its members to advise corporates on how to design more inviting workspaces, ten of which are already planned for construction.

[Links] Web: **sanktoberholz.de** Facebook: **sanktoberholz** Twitter: **@oberholz** Instagram: **oberholz**

Face of the Space:

As the coworking manager for both St. Oberholz locations, Tobias Kremkau has been overseeing the needs of St. Oberholz members since January 2016. His unique role gives him an intimate understanding of the day-to-day workings of café culture and of what drives expats and entrepreneurs to seek out creative environments.

St Oberholz
DAS
LEBEN
IST
KEIN
PONY
LEGE
NICHT
ALLE
EIER
IN

Hier wächst
Hier wächst

[Name]

Unicorn.AEG Courtyards

[Address] Voltastraße 6, 13355 Berlin

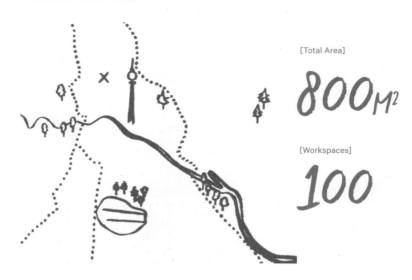

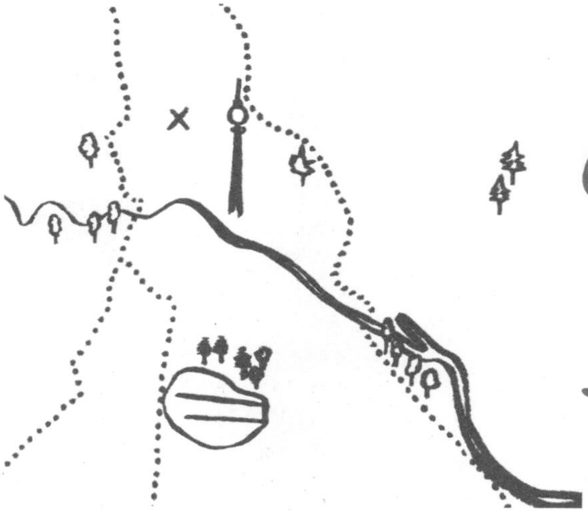

[Total Area]

800M²

[Workspaces]

100

[The Story]

AEG courtyards is the latest location in the Unicorn Berlin coworking chain, with five others located around the Greater Berlin area. The 120-year-old building first served as HQ for Allgemeine Elektricitäts Gesellschaft, the first electricity company in Germany. The building's nineteenth-century exterior is a striking contrast to the interior, which is bright and new with high ceilings. CEO and cofounder Florian Kosak says that Unicorn specifically chooses locations that are not your typical coworking spaces. "Our idea is to have a real place for startups, so our spaces – six and counting – are not so huge and posh, which means we can make our coworking prices up to thirty percent cheaper than many other spaces." The AEG location comes with a courtyard that gives ample sunlight to a lush herb and vegetable garden, which is used by Unicorn's own central kitchen in preparing soups, sandwiches, croissants and smoothies to distribute to all six spaces.

Even though startups can grab a workspace for a very low price, Unicorn doesn't scrimp on providing ultra-modern workspaces with everything you need to have a productive day. "We don't want a boring coffee machine on our premises," Florian says, "so we have a real barista to serve gourmet coffees, free of charge." When a bit of R&R is needed, there are also Snooze Tents positioned throughout the space so you can sneak in a nap.

[Links] Web: unicorn.berlin Facebook: unicorncoworking Twitter: @UnicornBerlin

Face of the Space:

Serial entrepreneur and Unicorn CEO/ cofounder Florian Kosak was born in the East Republic of Berlin. When the wall came down, his school curriculum changed from socialism to capitalism overnight and inspired his curiosity in business.

[Name] # WeWork Sony Center

[Address] Kemperplatz 1, 10785 Berlin

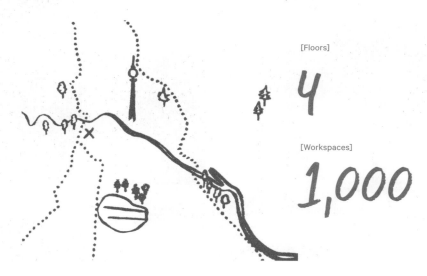

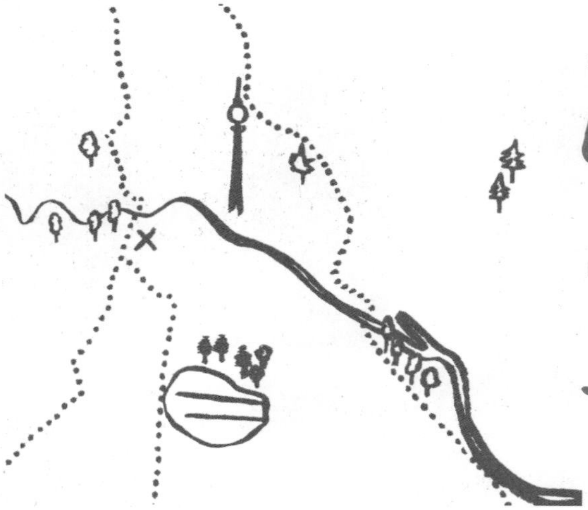

[Floors] 4

[Workspaces] 1,000

[The Story] WeWork Sony Center is located in vibrant Potsdamer Platz with stunning views across Tiergarten and the city. It offers four floors of unique and modern open-plan spaces and a selection of private spaces. Startups and corporates, both large and small, mingle with each other here without being segregated. Each floor comes with its own kitchen (and a limitless supply of free coffee and tea), lounge areas and soundproof booths for uninterrupted phone calls, while the main floor is a huge event space. WeWork Sony Center also offers yoga hours, breakfasts, haircut appointments, networking events and parties.

Community Manager Aimara Geissler and her colleagues make sure that everyone who walks through the door is personally welcomed and made to feel at home. "It's our mission to really get to know the members on a personal level so we can connect them to each other, make the right gifts for their birthday or anniversary, and get our events and wellness offers right." WeWork Sony Center is part of the WeWork global network of spaces, so members have access to all locations, including in Australia, Brazil, India and the US. WeWork focuses on flexibility, so members have many options available from hot desks to small rooms or entire floors for larger companies. And take note: dogs are welcome as the team at WeWork considers themselves dog-crazy.

[Links] Web: **wework.com** Facebook: **WeWorkGermany** Twitter: **@WeWorkGermany**

Face of the Space:

Community Manager Aimara Geissler is originally from Lisbon but her startup journey took her to Berlin. She was initially a member of WeWork but was so enamored with the homey feel of the space that when the opportunity to work there arose, she took it.

WALKINS
WELCOME
wework

exp

erts

inspire

Stefan Holst / Airbus BizLab

BizLab Coach and Program Lead

Stefan Holst has been working with Airbus for ten years. Two and a half years ago, he became a coach in the Airbus BizLab Hamburg, an accelerator focused on the aerospace industry, and took over the lead of the Acceleration Program in 2018.

"Airbus is a huge company," says Stefan. "We have more than 130,000 employees around the world, and it's operating in a complex industry. That can make it a tricky market for a startup: You've got a lot of regulations, you need expert knowledge and you need to know the right people. That's one of the reasons Airbus launched the BizLab initiative, to benefit from the innovation of startups and the way they work and to help connect them to the big corporates."

While a big industry might seem like an attractive target for a new business, it can be hard to get a foothold in a space with established giants and a lot of regulatory hurdles. In the aerospace industry, strict rules govern any product that's directly installed on a plane. This can mean that your idea will be difficult to ever test out, and it can dramatically limit even the kinds of companies that will partner with you. You're likely to encounter similar challenges in any other industry that touches on public safety.

If you find yourself struggling in an established industry, the first thing to do is find your niche. Try to find a single use case for your product that would provide a larger corporation with something it lacks, and then find someone at that company and win them over. It could be someone used to working with startups or simply someone in the department most relevant to your product – either way, you need a friend who can speak the company's language.

Another option is to "work around" regulations. For a product to be installed on a plane, it must first go through an intense regulatory process, but that same product – or at least, the underlying concept – can often be tested in a less hazardous context, giving you time to refine it and generate interest.

Airbus' BizLab Acceleration Program is focused on connecting startups in the aerospace industry with the kinds of established businesses they want as clients. Participating startups are put through a six-month accelerator with checkpoints every two months. The whole time,

Most important tips for startups:

- **Find your niche:** In a hard-to-break-into industry, figure out one perfect use for your product – something that will bring a significant benefit – and get someone to see it. Once one company takes a chance on you, other clients will be more comfortable.

- **Fake it till you make it:** Your innovation in aerodynamics might be intended for planes, but if you can test it on a car, you'll be able to develop your product without hitting regulatory hurdles. That can help you attract a partner to go the next step.

- **Your network counts:** The hardest part of breaking into a new industry is often just not knowing who you need to know. Try to build your network out so you'll be aware of your potential customers' needs and who to talk to about them.

they work alongside intrapreneurial teams from within Airbus, giving them a chance to build their first connections. Startups are paired with coaches who help them find clients, build their networks and learn best-practice business methodologies.

"Every two months, there's a focused review with the coaches and potential customers," explains Stefan. "The first one is dedicated to understanding the customer's desires – it's important for us to identify use cases. The second is dedicated to the technical feasibility of product development and its risk assessment and validation. The last is dedicated to the business viability: checking whether there's a sustainable business model and whether it can be extended to other industrial areas.

"On top of that, we've got a huge demo day at the end of each season to give additional visibility to the startup. And if a proof of concept meets internal needs, we're willing to give equity-free cash funding of up to €50,000."

In BizLab Hamburg's "Season #2," it started working with a Spanish/German company called Inflight VR that made a virtual-reality platform for in-flight entertainment. Airbus helped validate its early-stage idea on its shuttle between Hamburg and Toulouse, and featured Inflight VR as a co-branded product at the world-leading Aircraft Interiors Expo and APEX events in the US. The product gained international traction, and the company is currently extending its services to airport lounges.

About

Launched in 2015, Airbus BizLab is the aerospace accelerator developed within Airbus where startups and Airbus intrapreneurs speed up the transformation of innovative ideas into valuable businesses. BizLab performs an important facilitator role for the startups by easing their access and exchange with the investor community and industry partners. BizLab benefits from the global footprint of BizLab accelerators in Toulouse (France), Hamburg (Germany), Madrid (Spain) and Bangalore (India). In its first three years, BizLab has reported interactions with around one thousand startups worldwide.

[Contact] Email: stefan.holst@airbus.com

[Links] Web: airbus-bizlab.com Twitter: @airbusbizlab

“Airbus launched the BizLab initiative to benefit from the innovation of startups and the way they work and to help connect them to the big corporates.”

START
ALLIANCE

Christian Herzog / Berlin Partner

Head of Division, Digital Business

Christian Herzog is one of the rare native Berliners. He worked at a few Berlin startups himself in the 1990s and, in addition to his position with Berlin Partner, he's also the founder of Start Alliance Berlin, the local chapter of an international network of entrepreneurial hubs. He works to shepherd promising Berlin companies through their expansion plans, whether local or international.

Two years ago, Berlin Partner conducted a survey among five hundred of the city's startups. The public-private partnership between the city senate and several hundred local companies wanted to know what challenges new businesses in the city were facing. The most common answers were attracting foreign talent and expanding internationally.

"It's hard getting doors to open in Asia or the United States, or even other countries in Europe," says Christian. "A lot of startups have gone to New York or London over the last few years thinking it would be easy. They assumed America would be similar to Germany or France, but that's a big mistake: they don't know anyone there, they don't know what kinds of costs or salaries are normal, they don't know how to reach investors."

Whether you're trying to grow into a new country or bring foreign talent home, any time your company has to work across borders it's going to be complicated. You'll need to learn how to plug into a whole new network when you expand abroad, and how to wrestle with visa issues you may be unfamiliar with when trying to attract employees from other countries. One of the issues startups cited in the survey was the three-to-six-month wait time for visas in Germany.

Berlin Partner helps your company with both of those challenges. If you're trying to hire a promising candidate from another country, Berlin Partner can get you a work permit within five business days. And when you think your business is ready to enter a new market, Berlin Partner has built an international network to help make that happen.

"When your company is ready to expand internationally, there are a few things you can do in your new target market," says Christian. "First, most cities and countries have their own economic development agencies and investment banks. If you reach out to them, they can often help you find public funding or connect you to private investors. You should also hit up all the startup events in the new city, and you might want to consider hiring a local consultant."

Most important tips for startups:

- **Look for a local expert:** Most big cities will have their own economic development agencies. These exist to support new businesses and will likely be able to help you get on your feet in a new place.

- **Don't make assumptions:** You might think a foreign market won't be that different. Maybe you already speak the language or you've spent time there before. Even so, you'll likely face new hurdles you didn't expect, from visa requirements to different marketing norms.

- **Use what you know:** These days, many local business development agencies have connections abroad. Before you start looking in your target city, check in with your local entrepreneurial network; they might be able to help you get started elsewhere.

"But that can get expensive, and you'll need to put in effort to build up your network in each city. We already have connections in cities like London, Warsaw, Beijing and Dubai, and we're finalizing an agreement with Los Angeles. They all offer programs that are exclusive to the Berlin startups we work with."

Berlin Partner regularly takes groups of startups to cities they'd like to expand into and introduces them to its network of investors, coworking spaces, incubators and potential collaborators. If you'd like to go to New York, for example, you can be one of the fifteen to twenty startups that it sends on its twice-annual delegations. You'll have five days to pitch your idea to investors and get the lay of the land, and you'll get advice on local legal and tax requirements.

Meanwhile, with Berlin Partner's Start Alliance, you'll have access to accelerators, incubators and other essential resources in cities around the globe. With corporate partners like Airbnb and program partners like TechCrunch Disrupt and WeWork, you'll hit the ground running wherever you happen to land.

"It's a new way of working," says Christian. "Five years ago, cities competed for every conference and trade fair. Now we're hosting conferences together – New York, Vienna, Paris and Berlin are hosting the TEP conference in October. We're well connected, so we can match companies with customers and potential multipliers across the globe."

About

Berlin Partner for Business and Technology is Berlin's service provider for growth and innovation, a public-private partnership comprising the city government and over 280 companies. The experts at Berlin Partner create networks with partners in the scientific community and provide information on funding opportunities, suitable locations and staffing options. Berlin Partner also markets the German capital abroad, for example with the successful "*be* Berlin" campaign.

[Contact] Email: info@berlin-partner.de

[Links] Web: berlin-partner.de Facebook: BerlinPartner Twitter: @BerlinPartner

“We can match companies with customers and potential multipliers across the globe.”

Harald Marx / Daimler Fleetboard Innovation Hub

Head of Innovation Hub

By the time Daimler tapped Harald Marx to head its new Fleetboard Innovation Hub in Berlin, he was already well acquainted with the startup scene: he'd ramped up a strategy consulting company with two founders and worked with the Berlin entrepreneurial community in the past. With the Innovation Hub, he not only helps push new digital products and services to the global logistics market but also helps new companies in the logistics space to gain exposure.

"Startups moving into a complicated field like logistics face two major obstacles," says Harald. "First, it's a really fragmented system landscape – lots of information is still stored on paper, and lots of things are done manually. Second, it can be very hard to access customers."

The logistics field offers huge potential for digital solutions to optimize business processes and provide more transparency within the system. There are a lot of potential clients ready to take the next step into digitalization, but many companies, particularly the medium and large ones, already have their own systems in place, making it hard for a new product – even a good one – to replace an existing solution or scale up. After all, your pool of potential customers will always be limited to the number of systems your product can easily communicate with.

Even if you're still nailing down your proof of concept for one client with very specific needs, start thinking early on about how your product could be standardized so that it can interact with as many different systems as possible. This can mean including more functionality or less. Your product might have a larger market if it's more versatile, or you might find that a simpler component of a complicated process can be made universal.

"Even while you have your customer in mind, think about how to make your solution as easy as possible to integrate into other customers' systems," says Harald. "We often see startups create yet another fragmented system. They come up with a number of small solutions that only work for specific customers, and they have a hard time scaling their products and standardizing."

Most important tips for startups:

- **Think big:** To grow your business in logistics, you're going to need more than a few medium-sized clients very early. Keep that in mind when you're designing your product. Try to make it as universal as possible from the beginning, and think of which parts can be standardized.

- **Be patient:** Breaking into a highly fragmented industry isn't easy. Many of the older companies will be suspicious of any new product, even if it might improve their operations. Make sure you've got the resources to stick with it for the long haul.

- **Find a friend:** Those same suspicions will fade away once your product has been proven to improve a single company's business. If you can build a relationship with just one industry giant, you'll have a foot in the door.

The other thing that can help is a strong network. If your product can grab enough attention and show that it provides a real benefit, other companies will work to get their systems to work with yours, rather than the other way around. And to get that attention, you sometimes just need a single big partner to implement your solution.

That's where Fleetboard's Innovation Hub comes in. The Innovation Hub keeps an eye out for exciting up-and-coming logistics businesses that it can help scale, either through direct partnerships or by making introductions within its network.

"I'm a true believer that innovation within the logistics domain can only happen with strong partnerships," says Harald. "And we have the best access to the logistics market through our sales network. We're a very good partner to scale with and bring new solutions to mass market."

When a startup has a product that might fit into Fleetboard's business, the Innovation Hub offers it the chance to do a paid pilot. The company has time to fully develop its proof of concept, and it has its first customers already lined up. For businesses that just need more exposure, the Innovation Hub hosts regular workshops with startups and customers. Founders can pitch to potential customers, and companies can learn more about the latest startup ideas and solutions in their markets.

One of the Innovation's Hub's recent successes was Nyris, a Berlin-based computer vision company that started out as a B2C company. Given a picture, its software could tell you where to buy a product online. The Innovation Hub found a use case for Nyris' software, using it to identify the parts of a Mercedes-Benz truck and provide up-to-date information on their technical condition via augmented reality. Today, Nyris is working with companies like Metro, Lufthansa and Huawei and was selected for the Microsoft ScaleUp program.

About

Pioneering connectivity for more than fifteen years, Daimler Fleetboard GmbH was established in 2003 as a 100 percent subsidiary of Daimler AG and combines many years of extensive IT experience in the logistics industry. The core business is digital telematics solutions for commercial vehicles. Fleetboard's Innovation Hub, founded in 2016, is a space for invention and creation. With big data, IoT and artificial intelligence, it works to solve the biggest pain points in the logistics and trucking industry. It's organized in interdisciplinary teams to ship new products and services for the connected logistics industry.

[Contact] Email: **innovationhub@fleetboard.com**

[Links] Twitter: **@FBinnovationhub** Instagram: **@fleetboard.innovationhub**

“I’m a true believer that innovation within the logistics domain can only happen with strong partnerships.”

Rowan Barnett and Mayra Frank / Google for Entrepreneurs

Rowan Barnett: Head of Google for Entrepreneurs Germany
Mayra Frank: Marketing Lead, Google for Entrepreneurs Germany

For entrepreneurs, a 'community' can mean two things: a network of like-minded people and experienced founders you can share ideas with, learn from and collaborate with; and a group of people connected to each other by a shared interest or passion – namely, a startup's product, platform or mission. Through their work at Google for Entrepreneurs in Germany, Rowan Barnett and Mayra Frank have garnered insights on both kinds of communities and on how startups can tap into them to help their businesses grow.

"When you get started as an entrepreneur, you have an incredibly difficult road ahead of you and many hurdles in your way," says Rowan. "Having both the professional and emotional support of a community of people that are on – or have been on – the same startup journey will greatly increase your chances of being successful. If you also pay forward and give back, it creates a virtuous circle."

Building a strong community within a startup ecosystem is exactly what Google for Entrepreneurs is working to achieve. It partners with local organizations, tech hubs and community builders from Bangkok to Mexico City, helping to support entrepreneurs around the world. Google for Entrepreneurs believes strongly in physical spaces for communities to convene, connect and grow, so it has built Campuses where entrepreneurs can exchange ideas in person, learn from each other, and take part in Google-led education and acceleration programs offering mentorship, practical knowledge and access to industry experts.

The seventh Google Campus (after London, Tel Aviv, São Paulo, Seoul, Warsaw and Madrid) opens in Berlin at the end of 2018. In addition to its current hub at its partner Factory in Berlin where it runs regular events, it aims to further boost entrepreneurs locally by bringing an array of deep programming such as Residency, a six-month acceleration program for growth-stage startups. It also wants to strengthen ties between the German ecosystem and other startup centers, and help startups go global. Its Passport Program enables all members to work from any Campus or partner space around the world.

Fostering and growing communities has always been important to Google because its own company trajectory was very much influenced by its supportive local network. "Sergey Brin

Google
for Entrepreneurs

Most important tips for startups:

- **Test things at an early stage:** Remember, a product doesn't need to be perfect before it goes out into the world. Test things early and don't be afraid to fail.

- **Get feedback:** Working in a bubble doesn't help anyone. Why not ask your local startup community or community of users for feedback to learn how to build a better product or service?

- **Pay it forward and give back:** As you lean on the community to help you on your journey, don't forget to help others as well. This leads to a healthy virtuous circle that everyone in the ecosystem benefits from.

and Larry Page met at Stanford and refined their idea in a dorm on campus, before founding the company out of a garage in Silicon Valley," says Mayra. "They greatly benefited from having access to the local resources and community. Google for Entrepreneurs was born in the spirit of wanting to give back to today's founders in a similar way and make that journey easier."

At the core of its community building is Google for Entrepreneurs' efforts to create more diverse and inclusive startup ecosystems open to entrepreneurs from all backgrounds and walks of life. It supports organizations across the world such as Tech Inclusion and Astia in the US, and SheStarts in Australia, helping to get more women into tech and coding, and empowering them to start and grow successful businesses. In Germany, it works with a number of partners such as Role Models (a podcast and event series featuring female role models), SINGA (an incubator for newcomer and refugee entrepreneurs), and RockItBiz (an organization that promotes entrepreneurial thinking among youth).

When asked what advice she'd give to a budding entrepreneur, Mayra says, "Test things out at an early stage. Be more daring and bold. Have the courage to go all the way even if you think you're not 100 percent there. This is especially true for the young female founders who often wait a lot longer before putting something out there because they don't think it's good enough. Don't be afraid to fail."

Whether it's a local startup community or a tight-knit community of users surrounding your product, one major benefit of having a group of people to turn to is the ability to ask for feedback. "Never keep an idea to yourself," says Rowan. "You've got to share it with others, and through that process it gets refined and you win supporters. Getting critical feedback early on is absolutely key for entrepreneurs starting out." In short: join a community, spend time nurturing relationships, broaden your horizons, give back, and grow together.

About

Google for Entrepreneurs partners with startup communities and builds Campuses where entrepreneurs can learn, connect and create companies that will change the world. It provides financial support and the best of Google's resources to startup communities that equip and help entrepreneurs grow, all around the world. Founded in 2011, startups in its partner network and campuses (which span 125 countries and touch over 400,000 entrepreneurs each year) have created over 44,000 jobs and raised $5.1 billion in funding.

[Contact] Email: berlin@campus.co

[Links] Web: googleforentrepreneurs.com Facebook: GoogleforEntrepreneurs Twitter: @GoogleForEntrep

"Having the professional and emotional support of a community of people that are on – or have been on – the same startup journey will greatly increase your chances of being successful."

Martin Wrobel / HIIG

Associated Researcher in Entrepreneurship and Innovation
Visiting Professor of Marketing

Martin Wrobel takes the challenges that startups face seriously – so seriously that he wrote his PhD at the Alexander von Humboldt Institute for Internet and Society (HIIG) on them, focusing on some of the issues new companies have with sales and marketing. He's helped several startups expand, and he's now a visiting professor at the Berlin School of Economics and Law, teaching marketing classes, including product and sales management.

You may have a brilliant idea – a concept for a product that solves a common problem – but not have the skills to build the company yourself. That's what Martin's been studying for years now: What skills do founders need to get their startups off the ground? And what can they do to fill in any gaps they might have?

"Once you've decided to found a company, you're going to need a lot of competencies you may not have expected," says Martin. "You'll need to have a set of competencies to deal with problems you've never heard of before. You're in a constant battle with uncertainty and can never be fully prepared."

Martin wanted to know what makes a successful founder, or team of founders, and so he spent two and a half years conducting interviews and workshops and reading founder self-assessments and external assessments. He came up with a list of nineteen competencies a successful founder, or founding team, has to have. They include a willingness to learn, resilience, perseverance, a focus on results, communication skills, strong customer orientation and analytical capabilities.

"When you're trying to convince clients to buy your product early on, you'll likely get a lot of negative feedback and face a lot of resistance, which you'll need to overcome," says Martin. "If you don't have skills and competencies like persistence and analytical capabilities, it will be really hard for you to understand the customer and what your product has to do to serve their needs. This is true for every startup at the beginning."

Most important tips for startups:

- **Make a list; check it twice:** Have a long look at the kinds of qualities you'll need as a founder, and be honest with yourself about whether or not you have them. There's no shame in realizing you have weak spots, and knowing these will help you find the right cofounder.

- **It's about who you know:** If you can't find a cofounder among your friends and family, start expanding your search. There's a wealth of resources for people looking for cofounders, and, given how important the founding team is, you're better off shopping around than settling for someone who doesn't bring the right skills.

- **Do your homework:** The startup scene has been growing for years now, and there's more research available than there used to be. Don't reinvent the wheel. Look around for established best practices before you make a mistake.

Don't think you've got what it takes on your own? Don't worry. That's what cofounders are for. "A lot of people have good ideas, but many ideas are more complex today than they were fifteen years ago, combining elements from different spaces and markets. You often need someone else to help you. Many successful companies include one business-oriented founder and one engineer to do the technical work."

The best place to start your search is among your friends and family members, along with people in your professional network. Think of what skills you have and what you're missing, then whom you might know who can fill in the gaps you identified. If no one comes to mind, you'll need to expand your extended network. Luckily, there are tons of ways to meet your potential cofounder in Berlin: Meetup groups like Co-Found Berlin often boast several thousand like-minded members and host regular get-togethers where you can look for your professional soulmate. And websites like founderio.com offer you online matchmaking services to make the search even easier.

While writing his PhD, Martin and several other doctoral students from HIIG ran a series of Startup Clinics where they'd meet with founders and try to diagnose what was ailing their new businesses. Some of the most common questions were about cofounders – where to find them and what to look for. Once Martin and his class finished their studies, they stopped hosting these clinics; however, HIIG still conducts and publishes research and blog posts and hosts events on entrepreneurship, offering a jumping-off point for any founder who wants to add some academic rigor to their business instincts. His university, HWR Berlin, also has its own startup incubator (startup-incubator.berlin), a workshop and experimental space for startups and those interested in creating them.

About

Founded in 2012, the Alexander von Humboldt Institute for Internet and Society (HIIG) researches the development of the internet from a societal perspective. The aim is to better understand the digitalization of all spheres of life. As the first institute in Germany to focus on internet and society, HIIG has established an understanding that emphasizes the embeddedness of digital innovations in societal processes.

[Contact] Email: martin.wrobel@hiig.de

[Links] Web: hiig.de Twitter: @martinwrobel LinkedIn: martinwrobel

"You'll need to have a set of competencies to deal with problems you've never heard of before. You're in a constant battle with uncertainty and can never be fully prepared."

KPMG
Neujahrsempfang
NEU GEDACHT
IMPORTANT
TESLA
DISRUPT
NEVER GIVE UP!

Benjamin 'Bene' Jetter / KPMG AG

Head of Business Development at Smart Start

Benjamin Jetter didn't start out in accounting; he earned his PhD in theoretical quantum physics. However, he found that this background provided the kind of technical know-how that auditing companies needed, and in 2015 he joined KPMG's auditing team. He's now the head of business development with the company's Smart Start startup initiative, a program to help new companies build the accounting capacity to grow.

When you have more customer accounts than you can realistically tend to, it might seem like a high-end problem; after all, it means that your business is finding its market and your product is in demand. But while a mountain of accounting paperwork can seem like an enviable problem, you may find your growth is limited if you let your financial control systems go untended too long.

"Startups want to be able to scale," says Bene. "But when you have a growing number of invoices, it's very difficult to handle scaling. If the financial control procedures you use at your company don't grow along with your business, you'll have trouble finding VC funding. You'll need to convince them you're doing well financially, and that relies on trustworthy record-keeping. You'll need to show potential funders KPIs, and they'll be annoyed if you aren't able to report them."

Bene says that while accounting may not be your first priority, it's smart to install a strong accounting team early. Your needs will grow as your team grows, and sometimes faster than you expect. You might be able to get by for a while with the right software and a lot of time, but eventually you'll need to hire someone to do it, either in-house or at an outside company.

KPMG's Smart Start program works with startups "from seed to speed," meaning they'll help you in all the areas of KPMG competence, including audit and tax advice. They'll even draft a business plan, sort out your ownership structure and figure out what to do with any IP you might have. Then, when you're ready, they'll help you scale.

The program comprises four phases: starting, growing, strengthening and transitioning. During the starting phase, KPMG helps you with your ownership structure, business plan and talent

Most important tips for startups:

- **Get on top of things early:** You may not think your company needs an accounting team yet, but you'll be surprised how quickly that changes. Have people in place to keep your paperwork under control before it begins piling up.

- **Know when you need help:** When your company's small enough, you might be able to take care of your accounting with a few programs; and when it's big enough, you'll want your own internal department. But in between, it usually makes sense to outsource your financial reporting responsibilities and focus on your product.

- **Find an international partner:** Eventually, you'll probably want to expand abroad. If you're working with an accounting company with an international presence, they'll already have all your financial records and be able to help you do that.

sourcing. During the growth phase, you'll be working with KPMG on your company's growth strategy: how to expand and what your product strategy should be. In the strengthening phase, you'll be improving operations, addressing risks your company has and working on your governance structure. Finally, the transitioning phase is about preparing for things like your IPO and wealth management.

Throughout this process, you'll be able to use KPMG's Scale-up Accounting technology, a suite of accounting services that grows in functionality along with your needs. From day one, it will give you the option of scanning invoices and financial documents with your phone and sending them to KPMG for professionals to tackle, freeing up your time to concentrate on your business. For example, KPMG has recently been working with a Berlin-based e-commerce company, providing it with the accounting services it needs as it needs them. "Instead of building up their own accounting team, which would need to be increased every time the company grew, they came to us and handed over their accounting, operational, financial and tax consulting needs. Now they can focus on their R&D and grow without wasting time on those."

"Our accounting services allows your company to focus on your operations without needing to worry about a back officer or about topics like tax, legal and audit," says Bene. "You can see individual reports in real time, and if there are complex problems, we can help with them before they become real issues." And when you're ready to expand, KPMG is all over the globe. "If you want to expand to the US or another country in Europe, we can connect you with our teams there."

About

KPMG is one of the leading financial audit and advisory services firms in the world. Its international network makes it possible for KPMG to offer clients clear and consistent solutions locally thanks to cross-border know-how. KPMG operates in 155 countries and has more than 174,000 professionals working in member firms around the world.

[Contact] Email: bjetter@kpmg.com

[Links] Web: kpmg.de/smartstart Facebook: KPMG.AG.WPG Twitter: @KPMG_DE_Startup

"Our accounting services allows your company to focus on your operations without needing to worry about a back office or about topics like tax, legal and audit."

Ann Rosenberg / SAP Next-Gen

Senior Vice President and Global Head of SAP Next-Gen

Many fledgling entrepreneurs still believe that startups fall into one of two categories: those that focus on their bottom line or those that want to leave a positive impact on our world. Ann Rosenberg, senior vice president and global head of SAP Next-Gen, strongly believes it's not about choosing one or the other; startups can do both. "Social entrepreneurship is something we're seeing more and more in the startup world today," says Ann, who has worked in startup ecosystems around the world with her global team. "Being a social entrepreneur doesn't mean you don't earn money. A business, of course, needs to earn money to become sustainable. It's more about having the mindset of a social entrepreneur and building with purpose."

With SAP Next-Gen (a purpose-driven innovation university and community aligned with SAP's commitment to the United Nations seventeen Global Goals for Sustainable Development), Ann works alongside a global network of researchers, accelerators, startups, thought leaders, partners and more than 3,500 educational institutions across 113 countries to support entrepreneurs in developing and building solutions that are innovative, impactful and sustainable. Whether it's striving for quality education and gender equality or eradicating poverty and hunger, the UN Global Goals aim to build a healthier planet and improve billions of lives around the world.

While technology has been evolving at a breakneck pace in the past decade, we're now beginning to get a grasp of the light and dark sides of its influence on our lives. Now, more than ever, it's crucial that entrepreneurs understand the wide-reaching implications of their technologies and take responsibility for the products and services they build.

For budding startups who want to instigate positive change but don't know where to begin, Ann has a piece of advice: "When you're defining your idea and business model, make sure that both are well-linked to purpose." In a new book titled *SAP Next-Gen: Innovation with Purpose*, Ann and co-author Bernd Welz provide insights about what it means to turn ideas into reality with a "purpose-driven mindset" and offer guidance for business leaders on how they can define their vision, strategy and technologies to cater to innovation that leads to a meaningful outcome.

Most important tips for startups:

- **Make sure your startup idea and business model are linked to purpose:** Startups and entrepreneurs need to think beyond the bottom line and work towards a goal that will benefit society at large.

- **Consider the current and future implications of your technology and business:** With technology evolving at breakneck speed and impacting every facet of our lives, it's important to take responsibility for what you build and to think about the rippling effects it may have in the long run.

- **Be open to collaborations across industries and disciplines:** For early-stage social entrepreneurs trying to get their businesses of the ground, collaborating with researchers, universities, corporates, accelerators or other startups can open up an array of opportunities for growth.

"To prosper over time, every company must not only deliver financial performance but also show how it makes a positive contribution to society," write Ann and Bernd in *SAP Next-Gen: Innovation with Purpose.* "Companies must benefit all of their stakeholders, including shareholders, employees, customers and the communities in which they operate."

A hurdle that many early-stage social entrepreneurs come across when attempting to transform a bold idea into a purposeful business is garnering enough support (whether through investment or a network) to get it off the ground and reach more people. Ann believes that collaboration can open up an array of opportunities for startups aiming to make a dent in the universe. "We're seeing a really interesting evolution where we're teaming up with corporations, governments, accelerators, citizens, startups and universities to jointly build solutions that benefit each partner in the collaboration," she says. "All of these worlds are being merged together because they all need each other."

That's why SAP Next-Gen has built innovation hubs in cities around the world. The idea is that through these hubs and initiatives, startups working towards a greater purpose can connect and collaborate with a diverse network of experts, academics, corporates and partners to accelerate growth for all parties. Ultimately, it's about fostering a more open conversation about how innovation can leave a lasting, meaningful impact on the world.

In Berlin and the metropolitan area, SAP Next-Gen includes a network of twenty-four universities (including Hasso Plattner Institute, a privately funded university founded by SAP cofounder Hasso Plattner) and accelerators like the SAP.iO Foundry powered by TechStars Accelerator and German Accelerator. These offer various kinds of support including educational programs, mentorship and meet-ups for startups and budding entrepreneurs who are building something that links with the seventeen UN Global Goals. "Through our community, I want to help startups around the world have an equal voice, regardless of where they are," says Ann.

About

SAP Next-Gen is a purpose-driven innovation university and community aligned with SAP's commitment to the seventeen UN Global Goals for sustainable development. In Berlin and globally, SAP Next-Gen connects SAP customers to academic thought leaders and researchers, students, startups, accelerators, tech-community partners, purpose-driven partners, venture firms, futurists and SAP experts. Their goal is to reimagine the future of industries and the intelligent enterprise, seed in disruptive innovation with startups, and build skills for digital futures.

[Contact] Email: ann.rosenberg@sap.com

[Links] Web: sap.com/corporate/en/company/innovation/next-gen-innovation-platform.html

"When you're defining your idea and business model, make sure that both are well-linked to purpose."

signals

Daniel Dierkes and Videesha Böckle / signals

Videesha Böckle: Managing Director and Founding Partner of signals Venture Capital and Cofounder of signals
Daniel Dierkes: Head of signals New Business and Cofounder of signals

Videesha Böckle and Daniel Dierkes have spent their careers working with entrepreneurs. Daniel started out with Axel Springer's Plug and Play accelerator, where he was an investment and partnership manager working with hundreds of companies. Videesha Böckle worked at ProFounders capital in London and Redstone, where she primarily invested in B2B business models across sectors and industries before leaving to cofound signals and spearhead signals Venture Capital.

When starting a new company, you're likely to be devoting all of your attention to the development of a product. You'll obviously want to be sure that you truly understand what your prospective customer wants, and that you've iterated and modified until you can provide it. One thing you might overlook, though, is the culture you're building inside your organization – and that's a shame, because it can be a powerful asset.

"Building businesses is centered around people," says Videesha. "One of the things an investor will look at is the dynamics within the core team and their first hires. What's the organizational set-up and skill set? Are the founders well aligned? Do they complement each other? How do they interact when asked difficult questions? What's their motivation short and long term?"

Cofounders will inevitably bring different motivations and approaches to the table, and if they aren't discussed and addressed early on, these differences can come up when there's more at stake later. If you're starting a company to fundamentally change an industry and your cofounder is doing it for the money, you'll have different priorities. Meanwhile, if you aren't good at handling failure together, your product development cycle is going to be rough.

"It's important to discuss and define your values together with your whole founding team, and get them down on paper," says Daniel. "Understand what drives the individuals you're working with and formulate your company's purpose in a way that's easy for all of your employees to understand and implement."

Most important tips for startups:

- **Talk it out:** It's always helpful to have different backgrounds and mindsets on your founding team, but make sure you're aligned on your company's values and its goals. Have a conversation about the kind of culture you want to create early on, and make sure to implement your choices as the company grows.

- **Hire the right team:** A lot of your company's culture will depend on the attitudes of the people working there. That doesn't mean you should hire all of your friends, but it does mean thinking twice before taking on someone who doesn't agree with your mission.

- **Make it official:** You might not think you need official channels of communication yet, but when you do it will be too late to set them up. Make sure your employees know they're heard even before they have anything to say.

One thing to prioritize is hiring the right people. Rather than asking "What do you do?" ask "Why do you do it?" This isn't just about their hard skills; it's important they have the right soft skills too, and that they believe in the culture you want to create and will actively participate in shaping it. It's also crucial to communicate your company's values and purpose, and to set up the means of communication before you think you need them. Make sure there are opportunities for your employees to forge connections with each other.

Videesha and Daniel belong to the founding team of signals, a new brand launched less than a year ago to nurture startups through their development. It works with startups in different ways, depending on stage and focus.

"signals Venture Capital works closely with our portfolio of enterprise startups to leverage the corporate ecosystem, sales access and data within our limited partner," says Videesha.

Daniel adds, "For our partnerships, we usually work with companies that can gain value from our association with the insurer SIGNAL IDUNA, for instance, by gaining access to our network or our distribution channels. We also have a coworking space, signals Open Studios in Berlin-Mitte, where we try to gather together people from different industries who we can have good conversation with and might potentially work with in the future."

"But it doesn't matter where the entry point is in the signals ecosystem," says Videesha. "We always try to have a holistic relationship with the people we're working with, so we're not only helping them or working with them on a particular use case, but also helping to introduce them to our network. We like to be a partner and create opportunities for the firms we engage with."

"We know that often between corporates and startups, incentives are misaligned, processes are slow and relationships are strained; that's why we created signals. We work closely with founders and gather their feedback to create a better platform, experience and network."

About

signals started life as an independent initiative of the SIGNAL IDUNA group, one of Germany's leading insurance services, as part of the company's larger plan to create a collaborative innovation ecosystem that helps founders create new products, business models and services using the benefits of larger organizations. signals is empowered by its sub-brands signals Venture Capital, signals New Business and signals Open Studios.

[Contact] Email: **info@hellosignals.com**

[Links] Web: **hellosignals.com** Facebook: **hellosignals**

"We want to create an innovation ecosystem built for and by founders."

Matthias Lesch / TAB

Founder and Managing Director

Matthias Lesch started his career with larger companies in the consulting and education space. After working with a few established giants, he got fed up with long decision cycles and the slow pace of innovation, and in 2006 he moved to Berlin to work for a startup incubator. Twelve years later, he's the Managing Director of TAB, a company he founded to help other startups connect to mobile users.

A few years ago, it almost seemed like you needed only a dream and a JavaScript developer to strike it rich. "App stores" were still relatively new, and it wasn't difficult to stand out in what was still a sparsely populated field. But that has changed: app stores are now filled with hundreds of thousands of apps, all competing for customer attention and making it harder for a new company to gain its crucial first customers.

"Startups that come to us typically have an app in the app store already," says Matthias, "and they've put tremendous resources and effort into developing a great product. But it's harder and harder to get user attention, and without that, your product can't build any traction. Your app can be the best product in the world, but if it only has five active users, it's still dead."

If you're building a B2C product, getting user traction should be one of your first priorities – even if you're 110 percent focused on your product. Without users, you won't be able to do any testing. The first step to ensuring this might seem simple, but it's overlooked by too many new companies: make sure your product looks professional. Double-check spelling, make sure the layout is clean and easy to navigate, and confirm that your descriptions are properly translated in all your markets. Next, make sure you're describing it in a way that will get it noticed. Brush up on your SEO skills, and think of ways you could formulate your product text that will get it to the top of results lists.

If you can't seem to make any headway even after you've double checked that your i's are dotted and your t's crossed, it might be time to get outside help. TAB helps companies grow their visibility and their active user base, ensuring that you're advertising the right way, and doing it through the right channels, to reach the right audience.

Most important tips for startups:

- **Check your work:** It may sound obvious, but mistakes, typos and mistranslations will really hurt your customer outreach. When you're designing your marketing material, make sure everything looks professional.

- **See and be seen:** A huge advertising buy won't help you if you're reaching the wrong audience. Make sure to tailor your outreach to the audience you actually want to sell to; don't waste money on advertising channels that aren't related to your sector.

- **Content sells:** The best advertising in the world can't save a product no one wants. Use advertising to find your first customers, but make sure to use those first customers' feedback to perfect your product.

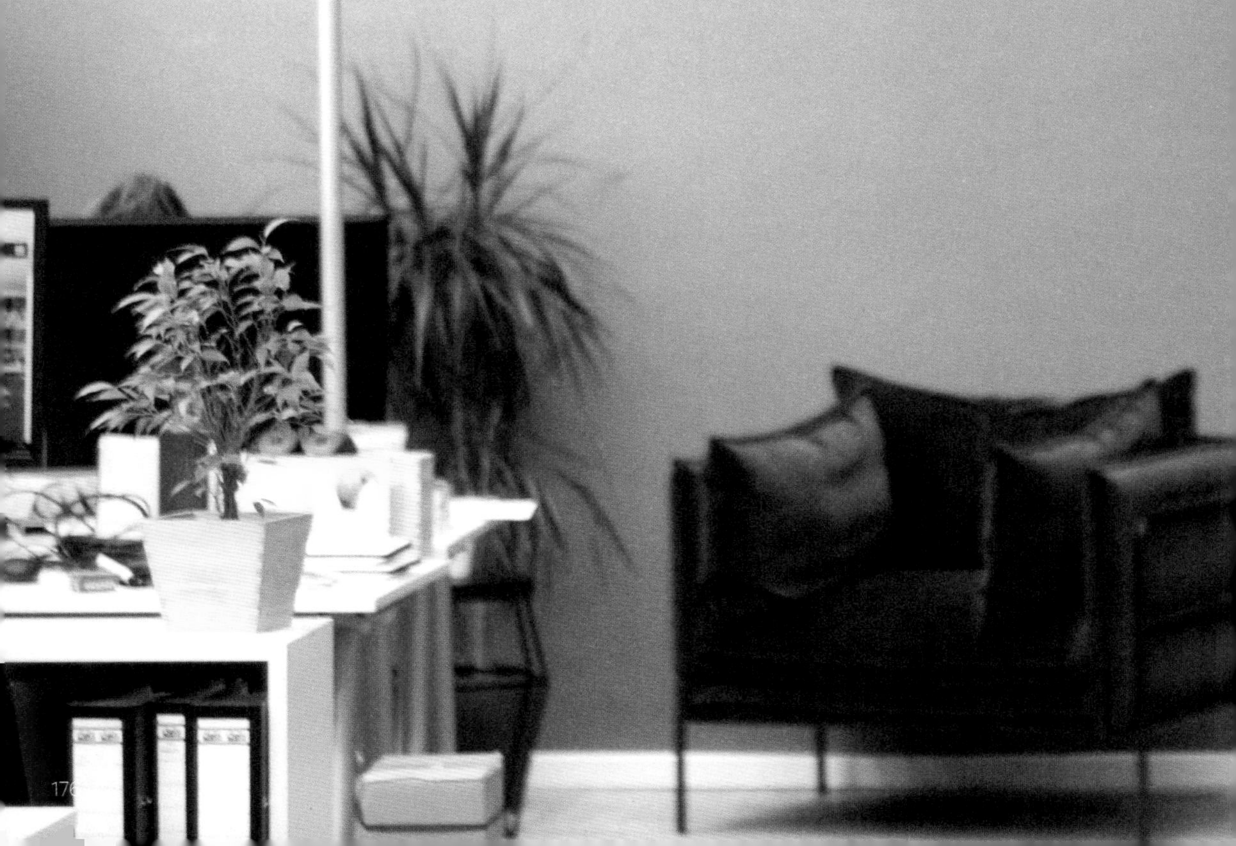

"We see ourselves as a way to outsource your entire marketing unit," says Matthias. "First off, we buy traffic in thousands of channels, so when a company comes to us they get an instantly diversified marketing approach. That's the first difference. Rather than work with thousands of marketing channels themselves, startups can come to one company."

TAB also works to make sure the right people are noticing your company. It ensures that your product is being advertised in the channels its target market is likeliest to see (for example, it won't bother advertising life insurance on a children's YouTube channel) and that your ads are in a format that best shows off your product. It also prioritizes advertising channels that tend to provide more active users, as you're better off with twenty active users than a hundred who only try your product only once.

TAB has worked with several Berlin startups already as well as companies like Grofers and Com2uS, a mobile game developer. "We've been working with them since they'd barely started on their game," says Matthias, "and we've grown our relationship as they've grown. They've grown their customers by several hundred percent, and we've grown our ad budget along with them. They're now a tremendous company, with hundreds of millions of dollars of revenue every quarter."

About

TAB is the gateway between brands and mobile consumers. TAB supports and enhances mobile media channels for brand communications by offering acquisition, tracking, reporting and optimization for campaign planning and creative assets. TAB's mobile experts navigate the ecosystem to provide a full 360-degree approach to the campaigns. With their in-house traffic solutions, they provide a wide variety of resources for their customers.

[Contact] Email: info@tab.company

[Links] Web: tab.company Facebook: meettab Twitter: @hq_tab Instagram: tab.company

“It’s harder and harder to get user attention, and without that, your product can’t build any traction.”

foun

ders

Benjamin Rohé

Cofounder / GERMANTECH DIGITAL

Benjamin Rohé has been founding companies since he was a teenager and has played a prominent role in Berlin's tech scene since its inception. With GERMANTECH DIGITAL, he's using his experience and his network to help build the businesses that will shape the future of Berlin's startup scene.

What does GERMANTECH DIGITAL do?

GERMANTECH DIGITAL is a company builder that aims to build the future digital businesses of our clients in a portfolio strategy over multi-year partnerships. We try to build at least ten companies at once in a given digital landscape, defined with our clients, and we try to make sure the companies complement each other – that they're all somehow related and add more benefits for existing customers and clients. And because we build so many companies at once, if one fails there's still enough leverage among the rest.

These new businesses are sometimes very close to our clients' core businesses, but sometimes very far. It's really about creating new revenue streams and new fields of business where our clients haven't been active before.

Can you give me an example of how that works?

We recently worked with EWE, one of the largest German energy companies. We've already started three companies for them, all in different fields. They're an energy and telecommunications provider at their core, but the companies we set up are not all in those spaces. One is actually a neighborhood community, like Nextdoor. In our research, we found that the biggest struggle in neighborhood community companies is user validation; but if you're an energy company that already has several million households and names validated as your clients, it's much easier to onboard them into a neighborhood community. So that's sort of the unfair market advantage we found over other startups trying to move into that space. The company built on data and customers that EWE already had, but it wasn't part of their core business – it didn't even have a business model from the start. It was meant to create enough traction in the market to eventually become one of the dominant players, even as the main business remains in the energy and telecommunication sector.

You've been founding companies since you were a teenager. What got you interested in starting your own business?
When I was fifteen, I freelanced for an advertising agency as a web designer; but when I found out how much they charged their clients for my time, I realized it would be smarter for me to charge them directly and cut out the middleman. So at seventeen I dropped out of school and created a web agency. Then I created my first tech startup, and I've been an entrepreneur in the tech field ever since. But there was no master plan or studies related to it. I didn't even go to university. It was just the passion and drive to create something on my own, and that's kept me going.

Since 2007, I've spent most of my time as a business angel investing in startups. Then two and a half years ago I decided to start another company called GERMANTECH DIGITAL. I sat down with my business partner Ludwig, and we thought, "If we build another operational company where we're involved in management, what do we want to do, and what are we good at?" We realized we're good at working with corporates and building companies, so why not combine those two? That's how we got started with the company builder.

We also run an entrepreneurship center located in the same space. That's something I created with our partners out of my university lectures and my work with all these different startups. I wanted to create a support infrastructure for entrepreneurs and innovators from all around the world to have better access to mentors, investors, and corporates. We also work a lot with corporate clients and partners on digital transformation and digital change, and help them interact with the startup scene and with founders. All of that is run by experienced entrepreneurs for the next generation of entrepreneurs, to pass on the lessons we've learned and the wisdom from the last twenty years in tech.

What do you think is important in creating an ecosystem like that?
We think there's a lack of access to partnerships, whether with other entrepreneurs, investors, academia or corporates. We wanted to create a platform that brings the three worlds – academia, startups, and corporates – into the same place. These three worlds speak three different languages, so the entrepreneurship center acts as the translator.

It's a very efficient platform, and we're able to bring interesting people – young entrepreneurs – together with those who have been there and done it to share their experience, time, mentorship and guidance. And we bring those experienced entrepreneurs into the corporate world to help innovate and create new businesses.

"People coming to Berlin come here to follow their purpose and their own dream, which makes it unique and special. You have so many passionate people in this town."

With all the startups you've worked with, what are some of the mistakes you often see?
I think one is not thinking big enough or giving up too early. It's something I see often when a startup experiences its first failure.

Also, not every business needs to be a venture-financed company. There are a lot of great ideas that can be run as capital-efficient and profitable companies, but many entrepreneurs try to make a venture case instead of making a small but profitable business, and they struggle with their business because of that.

You've been working in startups your whole life. What do you like or dislike about the lifestyle?
I think the grass is always greener on the other side. I remember when my first company filed for an IPO, all my friends who were with me at school were saying, "Oh, this is so great. I want to be like you. I want to do this." But I was looking at them partying every day and hanging out in the sun and enjoying life, and I was like, "Yeah, but your lifestyle is pretty neat too!" I think it's very difficult to see that. It's a big sacrifice going for the entrepreneurship life. It definitely has the benefits of being your own boss and making your own decisions, but it comes with a great responsibility for yourself and your employees. It comes with sleepless nights, a lot of hours in the office, and a lot of crazy travel. So I think the freedom and lifestyle are often over-rated when it comes to entrepreneurship.

I remember in the late '90s when all the investment bankers went into the tech world because they thought they'd become rich faster than if they stayed in investment banking. They were wrong, because you really have to be in for the long game.

When you really love what you do, you don't see it as work as much as if you were employed somewhere, but you still work two or three times as much as someone at a regular job. You age faster, definitely.

When you're building new businesses for companies, what are some of the assets they often undervalue?
Definitely data. I spent three weeks last year on a speaker journey through the United States. I was in eight different cities to talk about how data is the new oil. It's the same situation in Europe, and I think everywhere. Companies don't see the value of the data they have, or the data they could gather, or how much they could do with it. It's the number-one opportunity for digital growth that they overlook in their day-to-day business.

How is Berlin as a city to found a company?
I moved here in 2001, which was the nuclear winter of the internet era. Everybody moved back in with their parents or went into consultancy or investment banking. And over the last seventeen years, I thought about moving away several times. But every time I listed the pros and cons, I thought Berlin dramatically beat other cities and other hubs.

In the end, one key thing for me is the mindset of people here. Most people coming to Berlin come here to follow their purpose and their own dream, which makes it unique and special. You have so many passionate people in this town, and regardless of whether people come from Russia or Sweden or Brazil, they immediately become Berliners. It feels like a very strong community of people.

And even though Berlin is in Germany, I always say Berlin is not Germany. It's a very unique place, and you'd have a harder time recreating Berlin than Silicon Valley. It's very strongly rooted in its past, and a lot of opportunities in the city have been created out of what's happened here in the last thirty, forty, fifty years. And that makes it truly international. In many streets, you can't go into a cafe and order without speaking English. Almost all startup events are done in English. It draws people from all over the world to the city.

From a startup perspective, availability of talent and capital efficiency are important, and in terms of both I think there's no better place to start your company than here. If you fly an hour and thirty minutes from Berlin, you get to the Nordics, Eastern Europe, Amsterdam, Switzerland, Austria, so you have a lot of talent you can draw into the city. Compare that to Silicon Valley: if you fly an hour and a half, you're either in the ocean or a corn field.

That's the biggest benefit. That's also why Berlin as a city grows so fast; people are coming here from all over the place.

[About] GERMANTECH DIGITAL **builds digital business models for its clients in a portfolio strategy, and delivers dedicated teams that become central parts of the future organizations. It doesn't just look after its clients on a project-by-project basis over a short period of time, but helps them grow over several years.**

[Links] Web: germantech.digital Facebook: GERMANTECHDIGITAL Twitter: @GERMANTECHD

What are your top work essentials?
Travel.

At what age did you found your company?
Seventeen.

What's your most used app?
Newton, an email client and calendar.

What's the most valuable piece of advice you've been given?
Don't take things too seriously, and don't give up.

What's your greatest skill?
Connecting the right people.

Kerstin Bock and Carolin Lessoued

Cofounders and CEOs / Openers

Kerstin Bock and Carolin Lessoued both started out in communications agencies, with Kerstin focusing on politics and Carolin working in the music industry. They formed Openers in 2013 together with their cofounder Niko Woischnik (founder of Tech Open Air, Europe's largest interdisciplinary technology festival) to approach professional communications in a new way: they wanted to create a communications and events agency that would actually help companies build connections.

How would you describe what Openers does?

Kerstin: At Openers, we facilitate the intersection of digital companies, and we do that at different levels. We focus first on international tech companies coming into the German market. We help them with anything related to event production, community management or media relations; we help them come up with a launch strategy; and we help them navigate once they're already part of the market. Second, we work at the intersection of corporates and startups. We help corporates to get in touch with the community and develop programs that fit their needs and their industry. Last, we work at the intersection of public institutions and startups. We collaborate a lot with ministries but also with the city of Berlin – we help them to get in touch with startups and to develop programs that help startups either come into the market or expand. So, we produce a lot of startup delegations traveling to different cities. We help the city of Berlin prepare a delegation to South by Southwest (SXSW) every year, we're heavily involved with a project called Asia-Pacific Week, and we did a roadshow with the city of Berlin last year to different startup destinations in Asia.

That's also where the name comes from. We're opening opportunities, whether that's for startups coming into the market, corporates coming into the startup scene, or public institutions interested in this intersection.

What led to the idea for the company?

Carolin: We just realized that communications itself is much more the intersection of different factors, including the offline interaction part and the community management. We're sister companies with Tech Open Air, one of the largest European tech festivals out there. This year will be the seventh, with an expected 18,000 people. It's a four-day festival, including a two-day conference. This, together with the experience Kerstin and I had back

in the communications-agency industry, is more or less where the idea for Openers evolved. We've seen more and more interest from corporates in the tech scene, and more tech scenes emerging. Tech Open Air is a great place to start connecting, but we realized these companies needed more help all year long. They needed help getting the strategy right, and they needed hands-on manpower. This is how we conceived of it in the beginning. We three cofounders – Kerstin, Nico and I – all had large networks of companies we'd worked with previously, and we basically started out of those personal networks.

How's it grown since then?
Kerstin: We signed one of our largest deals pretty early with IBM. We've been helping IBM dive into the startup scene since 2014, when our company was not even a year old, which was a nice gig to show off in the beginning. Right now, it's just great to see that all the things we did at the beginning, including helping those foreign companies enter the market, have really worked out. We've been working with Kickstarter, for example, to develop its German comms strategy for about two and a half years now, and we've been doing the same for Eventbrite, the largest ticketing platform, for a year and a half. We launched Quora last year in Germany, we used to work with Twilio, and we've been involved with Pipedrive, Wayra and the like for many years. We also work with Atomico, which is basically the largest European tech-investment fund. We help them with comms and their events business but also make connections in our networks and help them find manpower on the ground, along with startup leads.

Carolin: We started much more with media strategy and comms-related things in the beginning, but we realized that the events part is becoming bigger and bigger. So right now, we also have a dedicated events-production team. We're not just organizing Christmas parties – we just did a big event in December for McKinsey, and we ran an alumni summit for Harvard Business School last year. You can see how it's events production in a way, but it's more about creating these opportunities for connection. The Harvard Business School, for example, brought the four hundred brightest minds together from the last few Harvard classes in Europe, and encouraged their networking and connections.

What have been the hardest parts so far?
Kerstin: This is the thing about the tech scene, or the startup scene in general: it's a fast-paced business. And we want to do a good job for our clients, but I've learned how important it is to also take the time to think about our strategy much more: Where can Openers be in five years? What do we want to develop for ourselves? The hardest challenge is to not get caught up in the operations side of the business, and to find some space for ourselves in this to see where we can grow as a company .

“Doing communications and marketing for your company doesn’t mean talking about your product all day but showing that you’re actually an expert in your field.”

We just discussed this week that we have this incredible, professional team that's growing in how they work and how they fit together, but getting there was also tough, for sure, especially finding talent that doesn't see themselves as just consultants but as business professionals. We want to employ a bunch of professionals who are really excited about what they're doing, people who might want to form their own companies in a few years. To find these individuals has been hard, but we have an incredible team here.

Where are tech companies failing in their communications strategies?
Carolin: It's important to think of communications in a much more integrated way, including all your business channels – this is what many companies miss in the beginning. In the end, communications and marketing are at least as important as the other elements of the business; communications and business development are strongly connected to each other.

A lot of companies probably think about it too late, and they also forget it's a lot of preparation. Once you're in the business and running your communications, you also have to deal with incoming communication, and you have to get your story straight and keep your communications consistent. A lot of companies underestimate how much preparation time that actually takes. It's a lot of preparation and asking the right questions, and really being an expert in what you're doing.

So, what we do for clients is a lot of agenda-serving, really being up to date when it comes to public discussions or discourses. Doing communications and marketing for your company doesn't mean talking about your product all day but showing that you're actually an expert in your field.

It seems like the old categories of "startup" and "corporate" aren't as clear anymore; so many large companies have startup outreach programs, or whole divisions run as startups. Do you think these traditional relationships are changing?
Kerstin: Absolutely. This goes for many verticals, too. Once we start working in a new vertical with a new client, we discover that there are so many layers to it. For example, last year we started together with Evenson, the official project office of New Mobility World (the Startup Event of IAA) supporting the German Association of the Automotive Industry (the VDA, or Verband der Automobilindustrie). We supported the event last year and also this year. It's something you see often; these days, it's really about intersections in different areas. It's no longer about the corporate world or the startup world. The mobility industry is one of the areas where technology is having the biggest impact, and these intersections are the only way they can really collaborate.

It's not just startups and institutions either. Larger corporates are also working on solutions together. Events is a big part of that, which is why we believe in offline get-togethers of these different industries and disciplines to connect them and build a solid foundation for inspiring and long-term partnerships.

What role do these intersections play in Berlin's startup scene today?
Carolin: This is at the core of our business when it comes to Openers and Tech Open Air. This is how we try to curate content. Look at the different verticals and industries, and just think of technology as the common element that changes these industries. This makes it interesting for us – we can work in so many industries. I worked in the music field, for example, and we're running a lot of music projects and working very closely with the music industry.

Kerstin: The project that I mentioned earlier, for example, South by Southwest, is at the intersection of technology and music. The same goes for politics. We've always tried to be at that intersection. We've always tried to be connected and stay connected with the city officials, and not just think, "Oh, these guys are really slow. We're bored." We want to know what's possible and what's perhaps not possible, given plans for development and change in the city. But that's what Berlin's about: there are so many people coming to the market who ask, What's the one vertical that's central to the Berlin startup scene? What's the scene known for? In south Germany, it would be mobility; and in Frankfurt, it might be finance. I guess Berlin itself has this one unique thing, and it's that Berlin can do anything and be at any intersection. It has multicultural teams and international teams, and it has this spirit. This is what we live off in the end. We have the creative industries – music, culture, the arts, technology – and it gives you the chance to be really creative. That's really important for us. It's why I came here and got stuck in Berlin – got stuck in a good way!

[About] Openers **doesn't consult; it empowers. Openers sees itself as a hands-on facilitator at the intersection of innovation. It helps technology companies enter new markets and opportunities, and it connects corporations and brands with the international startup community. It creates out-of-the-box communication campaigns, unique event experiences and challenging innovation strategies.**

[Links] Web: **opnrs.com** Facebook: **Openers** Twitter: **@OPNRS** Instagram: **opnrs**

What are your top work essentials?
Feeling comfy. We're living the cliché – an office loft and loads of plants.

At what age did you found your company?
Kerstin: Twenty-five. Carolin: Twenty-six.

What are your most used apps?
Instagram and WhatsApp.

What's the most valuable piece of advice you've been given?
Don't be afraid of opening up. A lot of founders are afraid of sharing their ideas.

What's your greatest skill?
We can be really passionate about our projects, but we're pragmatic at the same time to get things going.

Maximilian Tayenthal

Cofounder and CFO / N26

There might not be an industry less open to innovation than banking. With an essential service to offer and high barriers to entry, the established giants have little incentive to change. Maximilian Tayenthal and cofounder Valentin Stalf saw this as an opportunity, and over the past five years they've grown N26, the first mobile-first bank, to nearly a million customers in seventeen countries across Europe.

What does N26 do?

N26 offers a mobile-first bank account for all banking customers looking for modern and digital banking. We founded the company because we saw that there's been a massive shift in user behavior, going from offline to online to mobile, but the products of the big European banks are super old school and no one is providing a great user experience. So, we started N26 to provide a very slick user experience, along with lower prices than basically any other bank throughout our markets.

What made you want to build a finance company?

It's not the easiest sector to break into. When we started N26, we believed – and we still believe today – that financial services is the area most ripe for disruption. If you think about it, we've had this shift in user behavior that I just described, but at the same time you still have these really old-fashioned incumbent banks that do business the same way they did centuries ago. There's been very little disruption.

If you look at the other industries that have been disrupted by startups and mobile technology, the real disruption has never come from the inside – from the existing giants. It wasn't the big travel agencies that founded Booking.com, and it wasn't Blockbuster that founded Netflix. There are many more examples like that. So we thought there was a massive opportunity here that traditional banks weren't going to take.

And we saw that the banking market is extremely fragmented, mainly for historical reasons. You have French banks for French customers, German banks for German customers, Italian

banks for Italian customers. We're the only ones based on one IT platform and one banking license, so we can take on customers from all over Europe. It gives you much better economies of scale.

How have you navigated a field populated by such established giants?
Well, there's a lot of fintech startups working with or around banks, but that's not what we do. We're really competing with the big European financial institutions. We want to win millions of customers, and that means we have to take millions of customers away from Sparkasse, and millions from HSBC, and millions from BNP Paribas and all the other big banks.

But it's important to remember we're more of a tech company than a financial company. That means three things: First, we have a brutal focus on the product and the customer. We've thought a lot about how we can provide the best user experience for the customer and how we can provide the best user interface.

Second, now that we have a banking license, we can introduce a variety of new innovations to fully disrupt the industry. So while N26 is known by many people for providing one of the best interfaces on the European market, we also have the most modern infrastructure on the European market. For example, we built a modern core banking system, which is kind of the main accounting software for a bank – ours is much more advanced than those of traditional banks, which use systems that are forty years old. We're hosted entirely on the Amazon cloud, which allows us to offer our services at much lower costs.

Third, we acquire customers at a fraction of the cost of other banks. We invest so much in the product that we're very much preferred by our customers, and we have five-star ratings in the app stores. All these things lead to lower customer acquisition costs, and we can pass on these savings to our customers.

What lessons could you draw from that experience for others breaking into established sectors?
One, I think you really have to focus on the customer. You have to think about the problem you're really solving. Today, with every feature we're launching and every product we're building, we're thinking about the customer. Is this really solving a customer's problem? It's important to think about that, because we've had to prioritize scarce resources and only spend money and time on the things that address the actual needs of our customers. So that's the first lesson: to really focus on the customer.

Two, I think you have to be very data-driven. You have to launch a product as early as possible and also get customer feedback as early as possible. Those are two of the very important learnings we took away.

"The real disruption has never come from the inside."

What have you learned from customer feedback?

Unfortunately, I can't be very specific about particular products, but I can say a few general things. One is that when we've launched in new markets, we've usually launched in several markets on the same day – we launched in Spain, Italy and France that way – and this drives you to want to make hypotheses and compare results. You might have a theory that one market will perform stronger while I might have a theory that another market will perform stronger, and then you launch and see that a third market is three times as strong than the other two combined.

Or sometimes you're totally wrong with your hypotheses and even your basic assumptions. For example, we were really surprised by the success of our premium product, a paid account with a paid card and additional features. We were also surprised by how well our international markets did. Conversely, we built certain products that needed a lot of effort on our side, but which showed much lower adoption rates than we'd expected.

What made you want to found your own banking startup?

Six months after launching our product, we already had fifty thousand customers. We were working together with a partner bank and didn't have a single person at N26 who had ever worked in retail banking – we were doing banking without bankers. Now we have a banking license, so we have a couple of people who have experience with traditional banks, but we're still a tech company. The majority of the people here work on tech and the user experience of the customer.

You don't need to be out of an industry to really disrupt it. Like I said before, it's not always the retailers that provide the best e-commerce stores. It's not the music industry that built Spotify. You don't need to come from the industry to design a new product. The skills you need to succeed in one online space are the ones you need in another too.

But you had a few "normal" careers before. What made you decide to found your own company?

Right, I had corporate jobs, legal advisory jobs, consulting jobs. For me, I really wanted to disrupt an industry. And founding a startup is by far the most meaningful thing I've done. There's a steep learning curve – it's a very challenging job – but in terms of impact, you can build so much more that way. We really want to build a bank that changes the lives of millions of people, and that's only possible with a startup.

Then, obviously, in a startup you can build your own team, and work together with people you really like. And a startup is such a fast-moving field. We started with an idea five years ago, launched three years ago, and now we have a bank with about a million customers.

Since leaving your traditional jobs, what have you liked or disliked about the founder lifestyle?
If you have an idea and found a startup, it's a really big bet you're taking – you and the people you found your company with – and if it works out, obviously it's super exciting. It's this steep learning curve, but also the opportunity to have an impact and disrupt an industry. If you look at the corporate world or consulting, you're getting paid a nice salary and you have much higher job security, but the impact you have is generally much lower.

Your website says you want N26 to expand to all areas in your customers' financial lives. What kinds of directions do you have in mind?
At N26, we want to become our customers' primary financial partner. We started from the base product, which is different from how most fintech startups do things – with the "unbundling" that's been going on for the past few years, many startups have focused on smaller, profitable niches. Banks used to provide everything, and lately startups have focused on filling in all kinds of niches, whether cross-currency transfers, investment, savings, all kinds of stuff. N26 is basically the only ones that focuses on one niche where no one was earning a lot of money, but we did it based on the hypothesis that we could find customers more easily for that product, and cross-selling would work easier afterwards.

We're our customers' primary financial partner and we have their salary and credit information, so to cross-sell a credit or savings product is pretty straightforward. It's what banks have always been doing, basically offering people the entry product and then monetizing by cross-selling products the customers need, acting as their primary partner in financial matters. It's not thousands of products; you have to think about what the customer needs. They want a place to store value, make payments, save; they want to invest, or to have credit, or perhaps take out insurance. But that's basically it.

I think it's fair to say we're working on products that improve our value proposition to customers throughout the markets.

[About] N26 **has redesigned banking to make it simple, fast and contemporary. It is one of the fastest growing banks in Europe, with more than 850,000 customers across seventeen European markets and over 380 employees.**

[Links] Web: **n26.com** Facebook: **n26** Twitter: **@n26**

What are your top work essentials?
First and foremost, build your company in a way that makes you proud. And work hard.

At what age did you found your company?
Thirty-two.

What's your most used app?
WhatsApp or SoundCloud.

What's the most valuable piece of advice you've been given?
Be obsessed by your customers' needs.

What's your greatest skill?
Ability to take intelligent risks.

Paula Schwarz

Founder / World Datanomic Forum

The World Datanomic Forum isn't a startup – it's a community of leaders in different industries who share data to benefit as many people as possible. Paula Schwarz founded it in 2017 after leaving the World Economic Forum to encourage transparent decision-making based on trust and facts.

Can you explain what the World Datanomic Forum (WDF) does?
The WDF uses data to form a neutral base for communication between people from different cultures, age groups and genders. It's an inclusive network to foster collaborations and synergies through data. We have meetings where people can discuss the difficulties they have with changing processes, for example, with intercultural communication. During sessions, members try to come up with collaborative and achievable goals, and afterward our members rate each other in a trust-based social network. WDF members support those who need help to really stay strong, innovate and collaborate with people on their team who might have totally different backgrounds.

Data is important to find common goals and maintain transparency and trust. In the long run, this is what creates partnerships and synergies. The trust-based social network is called the "cloud nation" – as in a nation state. We say that our values follow us everywhere we go. We're led by certain core beliefs: (1) Everyone is a citizen of the world; (2) When we wake up in the morning, we all want to live another day; (3) It is wrong to produce things that were designed to kill people; (4) When we compete, we lose energy; when we work together, we can create more energy; (5) Because we can have everything, we have to learn to let go.

People understand that you need support to drive extreme innovation. The aim of the WDF is to promote peace and a more peaceful society through technology and data rather than one-sided profit-making.

Can you give me some examples of how you help people understand data?
Berlin has a very diverse working culture. For one thing, different generations work together. In the banking industry, a lot of people don't understand how cryptocurrencies work, and it can help if you show employees what's happened and how the banking industry used to work before the whole blockchain and cryptocurrency movement began. But we also help to frame problems and try to be more playful with them. Unfortunately, we're dealing with a lot of topics that are off the record, so I can't talk about them too much. But one is how we shift from fossil energy sources to wind or solar energy. We work with a couple of large companies that need to train their salespeople to sell wind energy instead of oil. Here, data is really helpful: you can show that oil doesn't really have a future and is not beneficial for the health of the earth. This is something we're doing with Siemens in Berlin, for example.

We're living in an era when there's so much doubt about common facts. How do you get people to agree on fundamental points?
Well, we all want to live another day, and all value peace very much. We all must eat. We all laugh. We all experience different feelings. This core understanding that people want to be alive is one that almost everyone in the world shares. In our events, we invite our members to dream freely. We also guard our members' confidentiality and don't give data out. We're not financially dependent on our members. If you can get people to approach certain topics with trust, they become more open to learning new things, because they feel safe enough to try out new options. We form mutual goals with transparent data to enable synergies. And we get the most updated data available. Data will always be wrong at some point or other, but that doesn't mean data usage is wrong as a whole. It means we haven't found the right attitude to deal with failure. We need trust and partnerships, otherwise we'll end up in 1984.

The company is still fairly young. How has the process of building it been so far?
The successes were very personal ones. I've been able to start living in a community that's very synergetic, that embraces trust and transparency and vulnerability. Confessing your weak spots is highly valued, so every day I'm in contact with change-makers who think about their actions in a very aware way, and who very consciously move away from this thinking that financial profit is the only thing that's important in life. If 2 percent of the people hold 98 percent of the resources on earth, something must be wrong. We're all missing something. In an era of isolation, we all strive for community, support and highly personal forms of success. For example, I'm allowed to work in a very creative way. I can express myself in the community in very different forms, be it in artistic events or our technical work or discussing whether

“We need trust and partnerships, otherwise we’ll end up in 1984.”

a philosophical approach to a project could potentially be harmful and why. We laugh a lot. We give space. We reflect. We continue. We grow, together. The subjects are very topical and inspiring for me personally, but I try to only be involved as "the Trainer."

Have there been any challenges?

I began writing about this idea, and suddenly the whole world reacted. I had this fundamental belief that if 2 percent of the world owns 98 percent of the finances, things can't change. So in an article for the Huffington Post, I wrote that someone should start something like the WDF. People began to react to the things I was cultivating and writing.

It's difficult to grow a field that's so new and to communicate with traditional venture capitalists and people who have been in business and private equity for a long time, mainly because such people are used to business plans. There's a lot of communication and trust-building needed for them to understand that this is something that's meant to be used in a synergetic way, and to invite them into the team. A lot of emotion comes out when someone's old reality is replaced with something so fundamentally different, even if it's positive. The debate about data doesn't include what it sets free for people if you give them opportunities. All this emotion. This is what games and colors and art are good for, and a loving atmosphere.

What are the current developments in big data that you're excited about?

Many young kids, myself included, used to feel like outcasts. So they sat in their rooms and built things that changed the world. Facebook is one of them. I was working with the Greek military at the Greek border with Turkey during the refugee crisis because of a project called Startupboat I'd created as a mobile think tank for digital humanitarian aid. There was so much death – people were blowing themselves up. On some days we worked while fourteen boats an hour reached the shore.

You get this understanding for intercultural communication and conflict management. Today, I often wonder why I had to see this human misery and what extreme wealth does to our leaders – and I'm only twenty-seven. So what if you're in a position where Goldman Sachs produces a business model for you, like Facebook, and you've not been trained to handle such extreme situations? We're now facing a new generation of leaders who were social outcasts. Many do not want to go into society.

I know how they feel. I'm one of them, and we need to stick together – empower each other.

At the moment there's still this energy of anger flying around, which you can see manifested in the spread of ugly "fake news," hacking, stealing data or "unorthodox" business models. You can start something legal but it's still sort of an asshole move if the company produces something that morally is really not cool. If we have a new generation of people who can make impactful decisions but don't feel like they belong, it means trolls and little gangster terrorists are running the technology. This is why I've invited my friends to come into the network. This is why we have the trust-based social network and try to find common ground in a relaxed environment – to basically say, "You're building something that will have a huge impact, and you need to chill out for a while. Thanks for coming. Have a drink, relax, and let us know whenever you're ready."

There's this tension that arises between corporates, which work in a somewhat transparent way because their shareholders want them to provide information that makes them trustworthy; and then there's this hacker sort of coder structure with people who are angry. All they've heard their entire lives is, "You can't do that," which is, as we all know, a direct invitation to do it. What we need is a new base of understanding and goal setting. As a founder, I think that a basic level of physical peace is something we can reach through money and through the logical and responsible coordination of goods and services around the world, be it energy, food, technology or education. A new type of goal-setting where we say we want to live in peace and we can do things that lead us there, whether you're working at Siemens and want to promote this change or working in the finance industry and don't think it's fair how profit is made. We don't say, "That sucks. You should leave." We see how we can work with you. We can show you trends and put fresh ideas in your head.

[About] The World Datanomic Forum **uses verified data as a base for synergetic, proactive and constructive deal-making and leadership of top influencers and high performers in Berlin and beyond.**

[Links] Web: **wd-forum.org** Facebook: **worlddatanomicforum** Twitter: **@datanomic_world**

What are your top work essentials?
Awesome people and my brain.

At what age did you found your company?
What company? We are a movement.
I'm twenty-seven years old.

What's your most used app?
Medium to write articles, and a lot of Adobe.

What's the most valuable piece of advice you've been given?
Follow your bliss, said Joseph Campbell. I love that.

What's your greatest skill?
My trust in my mission.

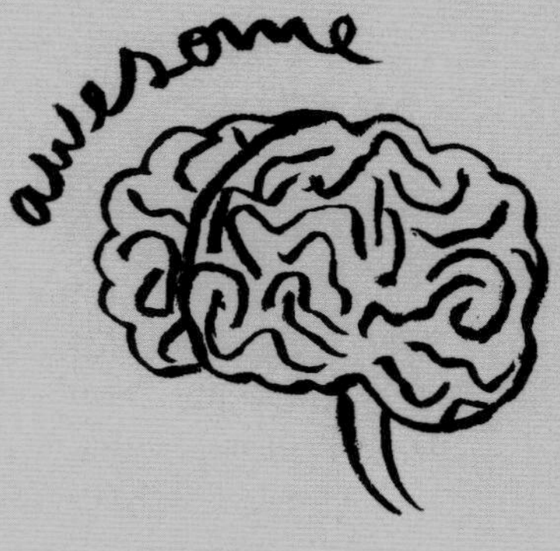

Sascha Konietzke

CEO and Cofounder / Contentful

Sascha Konietzke has worked in tech for over a decade, both with larger corporates and as the head of his own startups. With Contentful, a cloud-based content-management company he founded in 2012, he's helping companies to create better digital experiences for their customers.

What does Contentful do?
We provide a content infrastructure for developers. If you've been in touch with digital content, you're likely familiar with older content management systems, or CMSs, like WordPress and Drupal. These systems were created ten to fifteen years ago for pretty simple use cases, like getting a basic website or blog up and running. Today, if you want to build a corporate website with intelligence and personalization, you need more sophisticated tools.

So we asked, "How should content management and delivery look for today's requirements?" This is how we created Contentful, where we're helping developers distribute content across many platforms while fitting into complicated workflows within larger companies.

What did you do before Contentful?
I had worked on a startup in the consumer space, but that didn't go anywhere. We had a few thousand users but never enough revenue coming in. After we closed it down for good, I was wondering what to do next. I considered getting an MBA or working for a big company again, but I realized I'd always learned the most by doing and trying things myself, so I decided instead to work as a freelance consultant and developer to make a living, and to get exposure to a lot of different projects. It was about the time the iPhone came out. Everybody wanted to have a native mobile application. I'd taught myself how to develop software for it in the previous failed startup, and there were no iOS developers back then, so it was an exciting area to dive in deeper as a freelancer.

Next to the freelance work, I was still hungry to learn a lot more. I decided to study by myself on the side. I was basically doing my personal MBA, reading a ton of books and talking to people to get perspectives on different topics.

contentful

Do you think the education system is suited for today's employment opportunities?
I think our universities in Germany today mostly educate people to work in a corporate job, especially the degree I did, which was a dual study program in cooperation with a large company. During the degree, they basically equip their future knowledge workers with all the skills necessary to work within a large organization. It wasn't as theoretical as your typical university program, but it wasn't catered at all to entrepreneurship or starting something by yourself.

How we work is beginning to change, though. The era of lifetime employment at a corporate giant where you work your whole career is coming to an end. Working independently or as a freelancer is becoming increasingly popular, which means how we learn might need to change as well. I realized that I could learn a lot faster by reading than by attending a lecture. Of course, I don't want to discredit my professors; I was able to learn from many brilliant ones while I was at university. However, I learned more by reading some of the best-in-class books and then experimenting with these ideas myself, specifically by trying to start my own businesses, which I found more educational than a regular university program.

What did your first startup do?
It was a del.icio.us for places in real life. We allowed you to tag locations on your phone. For example, as a surfer looking for a great surfing spot, we let you discover bookmarks of surfing spots in the real world left by other users. You could follow other users or discover places by searching for tags.

Why do you think it didn't catch on?
We made some of the typical mistakes – there weren't as many public best practices in those days about how to build a startup. We locked ourselves in the basement for twelve to eighteen months without getting enough feedback and then wondered, "Where are the users?"

I would also add that in those early days of mobile, GPS and other location sensors were still really, really slow. When you wanted to tag your location, it took your phone a minute to find where you really were. That was annoying. You wanted to just press a button to leave a bookmark, but your friends had to wait for you while you stared at your phone.

With Contentful, we followed the lean startup and customer-discovery processes that I learned about next to my work as a freelancer. Contentful is providing services to businesses, and from early on it had much more revenue than the previous consumer startup. It was tough to be successful with an ad-based model, as we had to become super big before we could make enough money to sustain the business. Not many consumer companies achieve that.

"The era of lifetime employment at a corporate giant where you work your whole career is coming to an end … which means how we learn might need to change as well."

contentful

What kinds of lessons would you tell other founders from your experience?
Do a lot of customer discovery early on, talk to your future users, and don't just lock yourselves in and brainstorm together. Brainstorming is necessary to come up with ideas, but you need to validate those ideas.

It's also crucial that you have a technical cofounder on your team. I've seen too many early-stage startups trying to get their ideas off the ground, and they only have freelancers or agencies to build their tech, which means iterations, experimentation and getting validation can only happen slowly.

I also think it's crucial – especially in Berlin – to have more startups that build products for businesses. In Berlin, there are a ton of e-commerce companies selling goods online and consumer-based startups, but unfortunately there aren't a lot of B2B companies.

From my experience with previous startups and the other companies in this consumer space that I saw growing up next to Contentful, you need to become super big to be successful. Your chances are small.

In the business space, you can charge a lot for your services. If you solve a problem a big company is having, they'll happily pay you thousands of dollars for your solution. There are also a lot more gradients in between. You can become amazingly big and be a billion-dollar company, but you can also build an attractive business without being the next Facebook.

What made you want to found your first company?
I was always interested in tinkering with stuff, playing with Lego and things, and I had a lot of earlier touch points with business fundamentals. For example, when I was a kid, I thought, "Can I increase my pocket allowance by going out and buying candy at the store because everyone else is too lazy to go?" So I'd buy a lollipop for 50 cents and sell it for 80 cents on the schoolyard.

What drove me to founding my first company was the time I spent in the San Francisco Bay Area. This was during the times when Web 2.0 became a thing. Twitter was gaining traction, and Facebook and other social platforms were growing in popularity.

Along with this, there was a lot more knowledge-sharing happening on how to build a startup. In the 90s, you had to know somebody personally to educate you on startup best practices like how to raise funding. But in 2005 to 2006, successful founders began to share their learnings online. That made me curious, and I started to use my programming skills to experiment with startup ideas.

What were the hardest parts?
The hardest part has always been getting things off the ground: finding the early market validation, and creating something truly valuable for your users. This part is more art than science, and very hard to get right. Challenges continue with scaling the company: hiring the right team, creating a strong culture, raising funding.

Especially for hiring – and related to the point I brought up earlier – in Berlin it's been really hard early on to find experienced people that have already worked in a B2B company. There were a lot of B2C people who were producing games or making social apps, but these are different skills to what you need for a B2B startup. So that was a gap we had to fill, both ourselves by learning it but also by relocating people from elsewhere.

How has Berlin evolved as a startup hub?
It has developed tremendously since I moved to Berlin in 2012. When I first arrived, I was attending a ton of networking events, and most of them still had a German vibe to it. If you went to some of these events, either technical user groups or startup gatherings, they were quite often held in German.

That changed in 2012 or 2013. Many people came to Berlin from all over the world, and it almost instantly became the norm that all these user groups and presentations were held in English, which helped immensely in terms of including foreign people in the ecosystem and increasing knowledge sharing.

In the last few years, there have been many successful companies that have raised lots of funds, and that has brought in many more people with specialized startup experience. There are real experts for different areas and stages of your startup now. None of that existed when I moved to Berlin.

[About] Contentful **provides content infrastructure for digital teams to power websites, apps, and devices. Unlike a CMS, Contentful was built to integrate with the modern software stack. It offers a central hub for structured content, powerful management and delivery APIs, and a customizable web app that enables developers and content creators to ship their products faster.**

[Links] Web: **contentful.com** Facebook: **contentful** Twitter: **@contentful** Instagram: **contentful.inc**

What are your top work essentials?
Setting and executing goals, which gives lots of focus.

At what age did you found your company?
I founded my first company at twenty-four.

What's your most used app?
I use Evernote heavily to stay organized.

What's the most valuable piece of advice you've been given?
That Contentful is providing lots of value for larger enterprises and solving their problems, not only smaller agencies. Which is now the core of our business.

What's your greatest skill?
I'm not sure if it's a skill, but I'd say managing to stay calm during the ups and downs of the startup journey.

Waldemar Zeiler and Philip Siefer

Cofounders and Chief Executive Unicorns / einhorn

Waldemar Zeiler and Philip Siefer are serial entrepreneurs and veterans of Berlin's startup scene. In cofounding einhorn, which produces sustainable and transparently sourced condoms, they want to "unfuck the economy" by changing how customers, well...

What does einhorn do?
Philip: We started out producing vegan condoms, but now we're also into consulting – it's "C and C," condoms and consulting. It's a weird mix, but the company has never been just about condoms. We're basically following our mission to unfuck the economy, and we do that both with products and consulting.

What does "unfuck the economy" mean?
Waldemar: We were a bit fed up with the state of the economy and what it contributes to global problems. Whenever you look at what's actually causing all the trouble – like inequality and climate change – you follow this spider web, and at the middle you see the way our economy works and how it's contributing to all that crap. So we said, "We're entrepreneurs and business people; we see each other as part of the economy. Why don't we prove to ourselves and to others that a fair and sustainable economic model can actually work, and that you can be very successful with it?"

Philip: So we started an experiment. We picked a product that suited us, and decided to unfuck the product and then the economy by proving that it's actually possible. Three years later, we're a profitable company with almost twenty employees. We don't have investors or boards, and we set up our brand in the German-speaking area without any money, which was nearly impossible. But once the big companies actually realized that something interesting was happening, they wanted to know how we did it. They thought, They don't have money, but they established a brand. They're trying a lot of weird stuff and apparently they're very successful.

FEMALE
FUTURE
FORCE.

How did they do that? They started booking us for all kinds of speaking engagements and business and startup trips, and we started charging a lot of money for that, because it's not our main business. But they kept coming, so we kept raising prices. Eventually, we found ourselves in the business of consulting.

So, next to condoms, you can buy all kinds of consulting packages. We hit a lot of price points: €35 for a year's supply of condoms all the way up to €150,000 a year for one-to-one consulting with one of the einhorns.

So in order to unfuck the economy, you produced condoms?
Waldemar: Isn't that funny?

Why did you decide to work in this niche?
Philip: Actually, that was partly strategic and partly just a coincidence. We wanted complete transparency in our value chain, and that's difficult for many products – a cell phone, for instance, has four hundred components. Making a value chain like that transparent is nearly impossible. We thought, "Let's pick a product that's rather easy." Condoms are really cool, because they mainly just consist of rubber. We originally thought it'd be an e-commerce product, so it was great: It's very light, you can send them everywhere, and the return rates are really low, which is cool for e-commerce. And then we got started, and it turned out to be a very cool product. It's still a small market worldwide, but it's working. And condoms are a staple good, so it's unconditional income for us to do other projects.

You've founded several companies now. How did you get into the startup world?
Waldemar: I created my first startup in college, and seven since then. I came to Berlin the summer when Rocket Internet started here. I began two startups with them and later with Team Europe. I'm one of the very early founders in Berlin's startup scene.

Philip: I started a company called Stickvogel while studying. We started off embroidering towels for companies like Ikea and turned it into a B2B embroidery software company within a couple years.

What made you want to get involved in sustainable business?
Waldemar: I think frustration. I was really frustrated with the way the whole startup scene works, this whole investment field. Investors really push you to make returns. I didn't like it very much at the end, and I got really frustrated after a couple startups, with all the pressure about VC money and scaling.

"It's not about your ego; it's about the bigger mission."

Business Punk
WORK HARD PLAY HARD
Slack
YIEHAAA!
INNOVATOR
AUF DIESE JUNGS HÖREN DEUTSCHLANDS TOP-MANAGER
CITRIX

I took off for half a year and went backpacking in South America, and then took half a year in Berlin to think about how you could start something with a positive impact. One day, if you have kids, they'll ask you what you've done about all this shit happening in the world. Up until then, I didn't have an answer. But my son is now one and a half, and I'm happy I can tell him something different now.

It seems like more and more new businesses are trying to operate sustainably. Why is it becoming a more popular business philosophy now?
Philip: First of all, there's a huge shift in how people work with companies, especially with Generation Y and the generation after. Those generations are really looking for purpose, and I think that's something really different. A lot of the big companies that visit us are really struggling to get them on board and keep them, because they can't provide purpose. So, I think that's a big driver.

Waldemar: I also think customers are becoming more and more aware of it, asking where their products are from, how they're made, who made them – that's also a generational thing, because Generation Y is the one that will be spending most of the money soon. So, I think different trends are coming together. People are really looking for purpose now. People don't just want to work in just a company – at least, not everyone does. There are still a lot of people who just want to work for money, but they realize after a while, What's that for? I spend most of my time working. Why am I doing this?

In these talks you give, what's the big headline?
Philip: The title is usually "Unfuck the Economy." Basically, we say that it's possible to be very successful, innovative and disruptive while maintaining some core values. We show a lot of examples of how we apply our three values – unicornique, fairstainable, and fight and hug – and we show companies how we apply them, and ask weird questions they usually don't get asked.

Waldemar: We question everything – we're like court jesters. We're challenging the kings at the big companies. And because we're so funny and nice and weird, they can listen to us without losing face. That's what they like. We can be really tough and honest with them, and still have a good laugh after.

What do those principles mean?
Philip: Unicornique means we want to do things differently. It's a mechanism to prevent us from doing normal stuff. When something's regular or half-assed, we say we're not going to do it. That's why we have our cool bags instead of the ugly packages you usually have for condoms. We try to do everything crazy.

Fairstainable just means that in everything we do, we try to be as fair and sustainable as possible. The bigger we get, the more we can be fair and sustainable; but even when we were starting from scratch, we told our clients what we were doing.

Waldemar: And fight and hug... Even though my cofounder and I look the same, we're very different; and even before we started the company, we didn't get along and had huge fights. So I told Philip, let's go to couple's therapy, otherwise we'll never be able to start a company; we'll burn out first. So that's what we encourage at our team. It's OK to fight, but before you go to bed you have to hug each other, because it's not about your ego; it's about the bigger mission.

You've founded so many startups. When is it time to leave a company?
Philip: Never. We're big fans of Götz Werner, the founder of the dm drugstore chain. He's still on board. They're doing 8 billion in revenue, and they have 60,000 employees, 3,500 shops, and he's still on board, and his son is following him. I don't think there's ever a good time to leave. Mark Zuckerberg is still doing his shit, and the Google guys are still on board. I think if you want to be really successful, you have to do that.

Waldemar: Too many founders, especially in Germany, are thinking of their exit only. They leave far too early, and they don't try without investors, which can also be feasible.

How has Berlin changed since you became part of its startup scene?
Waldemar: In the beginning, it was very hard to get funding, seed money and Series A, which is completely different now. If your idea is not too bad, you'll have no problem getting business investment or Series A. Though I'm not a huge fan of investment anymore, it's easier.

There are also many more founders around. In the beginning, when I started, there were only the Samwer brothers at Alando and later Jamba, the other startups their employees founded. They were all from this one university. But it was pretty boring; it was just copycats of US businesses and there wasn't much money.

Now it's really different. It's not just copycats and e-commerce. Soundcloud was created, so it's a different story now. Now there are more different startups and more international people.

[About] **einhorn is a Berlin-based vegan condom company that's turning into a consulting company, and will probably one day win the first Nobel peace prize awarded to a for-profit company for their achievements in unfucking the economy.**

[Links] Web: einhorn.my Facebook: einhorn.berlin Twitter: @EinhornBerlin Instagram: einhorn.berlin

What are your top work essentials?
Waldemar and Philip: Non-violent communication.

At what age did you found your company?
Waldemar: Eighteen.
Philip: Around twenty-five, twenty-six.

What's your most used app?
Waldemar: Either email or the weather app.
Philip: Insta baby.

What's the most valuable piece of advice you've been given?
Waldemar: Relax.
Philip: Green asparagus sprinkled with olive oil and put on the grill is awesome.

What's your greatest skill?
Waldemar: I'm a meta person. I can see things from outside my own perspective.
Philip: I didn't grow up.

directory

Startups

Assistr Digital Health Systems GmbH
c/o Factory Works GmbH
Lohmühlenstraße 65
Berlin 12435
assistrcare.com

BigchainDB GmbH
Chausseestraße 19
10115 Berlin
bigchaindb.com

Bunch / 12grapes GmbH
Invalidenstr. 112
10115 Berlin
bunch.ai

Codepan GmbH
8B Paul-Lincke-Ufer,
10999 Berlin
codepan.com

Coworkies
Factory Görlitzer Park
Lohmühlenstraße 65
12435 Berlin
coworkies.com

GlassDollar
Gärtnerstraße 28
10245 Berlin
glassdollar.com

Green City Solutions GmbH
EUREF-Campus 7–8
Berlin 10829
greencitysolutions.de

Grover
Holzmarktstraße 11
Berlin 10179
getgrover.com

Infarm GmbH
Glogauerstraße 6
Berlin 10999
infarm.com

Jaspr
Emser Straße 28
Berlin 12051
jasprtrades.com

Kontist GmbH
Torstraße 177
Berlin 10115
kontist.com

Programs

APX Axel Springer Porsche GmbH & Co. KG
Markgrafenstraße 12–14
10969 Berlin
apx.ac

Beyond1435
Krausenstraße 9-10
10117 Berlin, Germany
beyond1435.com

enpact e.v.
Gleimstraße 50
Berlin 10437
Enpact.org

METRO Accelerator
Breite Str. 1
Berlin 10178
metroaccelerator.com

Next Big Thing AG
(c/o Factory Works GmbH)
Lohmühlenstraße 65
Berlin 12435
nextbigthing.ag

Plug and Play Berlin
Krausenstraße 9-10
10117 Berlin
pnptc.com

SAP.iO Foundry Berlin
Stresemannstraße 123
Berlin 10963
sap.io

SAP IoT Startup Accelerator
Rosenthaler Straße 38
10178 Berlin
sap.com/iot-startup

Techstars Berlin
Breite Str. 1, 10178 Berlin
techstars.com/programs/berlin-program

Wincubator
EUREF Campus 10-11
10829 Berlin
wincubator.com

Spaces

Ahoy! Berlin
Wattstraße 11
13355 Berlin
ahoyberlin.com

betahaus GmbH
Prinzessinnenstraße 19–20
Berlin 10969
betahaus.com

Fab Lab Berlin
Prenzlauer Allee 242
10405 Berlin
fablab.berlin

Factory Görlitzer Park
Lohmühlenstraße 65
Berlin 12435
factoryberlin.com

Google for Entrepreneurs hub
Factory Berlin Görlitzer Park
Lohmühlenstraße 65
12435 Berlin
campus.co/berlin

KAOS Berlin
Wilhelminenhofstraße 92
Berlin 12459
kaosberlin.de

Mindspace
Skalitzer Straße 104
Berlin-Kreuzberg 10997
mindspace.me

Silicon Allee
Chausseestraße 19,
10115 Berlin
siliconallee.com

St. Oberholz
Rosenthaler Straße 72a
10119 Berlin
sanktoberholz.de

Unicorn.AEG Courtyards
Voltastraße 6
13355 Berlin
unicorn.berlin

WeWork Sony Center
Kemperplatz 1
Berlin 10785
wework.com

Experts

Airbus BizLab Toulouse
57 Avenue Jean Monnet
31770 Colomiers
France
airbus-bizlab.com

Berlin Partner
Fasanenstraße 85
10623 Berlin
berlin-partner.de

Daimler Fleetboard Innovation Hub
Wattstraße 11
13355 Berlin
innovationhub.fleetboard.com

Google for Entrepreneurs hub at Factory Görlitzer Park
Lohmühlenstraße 65
12435 Berlin
googleforentrepreneurs.com
campus.co/berlin

HIIG (Alexander von Humboldt Institute for Internet and Society)
Französische Straße 9
10117 Berlin
hiig.de

KPMG AG Wirtschaftsprüfungsgesellschaft
Klingelhöferstraße 18
10785 Berlin
kpmg.de/smartstart

SAP Next-Gen BER03
Rosenthaler Straße 30
10178 Berlin
sap.com

signals
Am Nordbahnhof 3
10115 Berlin
hellosignals.com

TAB
Potsdamer Straße 91
10785 Berlin
tab.company

Founders

Contentful
Ritterstraße 12–14
10969 Berlin
contentful.com

einhorn products GmbH
Skalitzer Straße 100
10997 Berlin
einhorn.my

GERMANTECH DIGITAL make a startup services GmbH
Stresemannstraße 123
10963 Berlin
Germantech.digital

N26 GmbH
Klosterstraße 62
10179 Berlin
n26.com

OPENERS
Usedomerstraße 4
13355 Berlin
opnrs.com

The World Datanomic Forum
www.wd-forum.org

Accountants

Barnbrook GmbH
Wallstraße 58/59
10179 Berlin
barnbrook.tax

Boersing Pohl & Partner
Lietzenburger Straße 46
10789 Berlin
boersing-pohl.de

Deloitte
Neues Kranzler Eck
Kurfürstendamm 23
10719 Berlin
deloitte.com/de

Frank, Follert und Loczenski Steuerberatungsgesellschaft mbH
Hauptstraße 65
12159 Berlin
ffl-berlin.de

Klier & Ott
Reinhardtstraße 52
10117 Berlin
klier-ott.de

KPMG AG Wirtschaftsprüfungsgesellschaft
Klingelhöferstraße 18
10785 Berlin
kpmg.de/smartstart

KWWM Kleppeck, Welbers, Winkel and Partner
Kurfürstendamm 179
10707 Berlin
kwwm.de

Lanza & Remuss
Grolmanstraße 39
10623 Berlin
lanza-remuss.de

Schürmann, Schürmann & Schürmann
Monbijouplatz 10
10178 Berlin
steuerberater-berlin-schuermann.de

Stein & Partners LLP
Ballenstedterstraße 16a
10709 Berlin
stein-partners.com

Zabel · Moellman · Gaigl
Fanny-Zobel-Straße 11
12435 Berlin
kanzlei-zmg.de

directory

Banks

Berliner Sparkasse
Alexanderplatz 2
10178 Berlin
berliner-sparkasse.de

Berliner Volksbank
Frankfurter Allee 69
10247 Berlin
berliner-volksbank.de

Commerzbank
Potsdamerstraße 125
10783 Berlin
commerzbank.de

Deutsche Bank
Friedrichstraße 181
10117 Berlin
deutsche-bank.de

DKB
Kronenstraße 8-10
10117 Berlin
dkb.de

Landesbank Berlin
Alexanderplatz 2
10178 Berlin
lbb.de

N26
next.n26.com

Penta Fintech
getpenta.com

solarisBank AG
Anna-Louisa-Karsch-Straße 2
10178 Berlin
solarisbank.com

Coffee Shops and Places with Wifi

Bonanza Coffee Roasters
Adalbertstraße 70
10999 Berlin
bonanzacoffee.de

Hallesches Haus
Tempelhofer Ufer 1
10961 Berlin
Hallescheshaus.com

Homemade
Simon-Dach-Str.10
10245 Berlin, Germany
homemade-berlin.de

Michelberger Hotel
Warschauerstraße 39-40
10243 Berlin
michelbergerhotel.com

Milch & Zucker
Oranienstraße 37
10999 Berlin
Milchundzucker.eu

Mirage Bistro
Reinickendorferstr 110
13347 Berlin
mirage.berlin

Roeststaette Berlin
Ackerstraße 173
10115 Berlin
shop.roeststaette.de

R/D
Chausseestr. 19,
10115 Berlin
rdcoffeebar.co

Shakespeare and Sons
Warschauerstraße 74
10243 Berlin
shakesbooks.de

Spreegold
Rosa-Luxemburg-Straße 2
10178 Berlin
spreegold.com

The Digital Eatery
Unter den Linden 17
10117 Berlin
microsoft-berlin.de/the-digital-eatery

WestBerlin
Friedrichstrasse 215
10969 Berlin
westberlin-bar-shop.de

Expat Groups and Meetups

American German Business Club - Berlin
Agbc-berlin.de

Berlin Expats
facebook.com/groups/berlin-expats

Berlin Expats Meetup
meetup.com/berlin-expats

Free Advice Berlin
facebook.com/groups/FreeAdviceBerlin

InterNations
internations.org/berlin-expats

MumsLikeUs
meetup.com/MumsLikeUs-Berlin

The Rotary Club Berlin International
berlin-international.rotary.de

Toytown Berlin Young English Speakers
facebook.com/groups/toytownberlin

Flats and Rentals

Berlin Apartments
facebook.com/groups/183048595060764

Cherryflats
cherryflats.de

Coming Home
coming-home.org

Flats In Berlin
facebook.com/groups/393237407451209

Immobilien Scout GmbH
immobilienscout24.de

Immobilo
immobilo.de

Immowelt
immowelt.de

Spotahome
spotahome.com/berlin

WG-Gesucht.de
wg-gesucht.de

WOLOHO
Woloho.com

Wunderflats
Wunderflats.com

Zeit Raum
zeit-raum.de

Important Government Offices

Ausländerbehörde (Foreigners Offices)
service.berlin.de/standorte/auslandsamt

Berlin Partner für Wirtschaft und Technologie GmbH
Fasanenstraße 85
10623 Berlin
berlin-partner.de

Bezirksamt (District Council Offices)
service.berlin.de/dienstleistung/120686

Bundesagentur Fülr Arbeit
arbeitsagentur.deuı
Federal Ministry of Economic Affairs and Energy
Scharnhorststraße 34-37
10115 Berlin
existenzgruender.de

Finanzamt (Tax Offices)
service.berlin.de/standorte/finanzaemter

Handwerkskammer Berlin
Blücherstraße 68
10961 Berlin
startercenter-berlin.de

Landesamt für Bürger- und Ordnungsangelegenheiten
berlin.de/labo

Service-Portal Berlin
Service.berlin.de

Incubators and Accelerators

Axel Springer Plug and Play
Markgrafenstraße 12-14
10969 Berlin
axelspringerplugandplay.com

Hackmind.ai
Winsstraße 62
10405 Berlin
hackmind.ai

Social Impact Lab
Muskauer Straße 24
10997 Berlin
berlin.socialimpactlab.eu

Startupbootcamp
Friedrichstraße 68
10117 Berlin
startupbootcamp.org

Viessman Innovation Boiler
Friedrichstraße 148
10117 Berlin
innovationboiler.com

Vodafone F-lane
Vodafone Institute for Society and Communications
Behrenstraße 18
10117 Berlin
f-lane.com

Insurance Companies

AOK Die Gesundheitskasse
en.zuwanderer.aok.de

AXA
axa.de

BVV Versicherungsverein des Bankgewerbes a.G.
Kurfürstendamm 111 - 113
10711 Berlin
bvv.de

Deutsche Lebensver-sicherungs-AG
An den Treptowers 3
12435 Berlin
dlvag.allianz.de

Die Techniker
tk.de

Feuersozietät Berlin Branden-burg Versicherung Aktienge-sellschaft
Am Karlsbad 4-5
10785 Berlin
feuersozietaet.de

IDEAL Versicherung AG
Kochstraße 26
10969 Berlin
ideal-versicherung.de

OKV - Ostdeutsche Kommunalversicherung a. G.
Konrad-Wolf-Straße 91/92
13055 Berlin
okv.de

Protektor Lebensver-sicherungs-AG
Wilhelmstraße 43 G
10117 Berlin
protektor-ag.de

Zürich Versicherungen AG
zurich.de

Investors

Atlantic Labs
Rosenthalerstraße 13
10119 Berlin
atlanticlabs.de

Axel Springer Digital Ventures GmbH
Axel-Springer-Straße 65
10888 Berlin
axelspringer.de

BY Capital Management GmbH
Blue Yard Capital
Grimmstraße 13
10967 Berlin
blueyard.com

Cherry Ventures Management GmbH
Linienstraße 165
10115 Berlin
cherry.vc

Earlybird
Münzstraße 21
10178 Berlin
earlybird.com

Fly Ventures
Ackerstraße 6
10115 Berlin
fly.vc

Hasso Plattner Ventures
Rudolf-Breitscheid-Straße 187
14482 Potsdam
hp-ventures.com

IBB Beteiligungsgesellschaft mbH
Bundesallee 210
10719 Berlin
ibb-bet.de

innogy Ventures GmbH
Hardenbergstr. 32
10623 Berlin
innogy.ventures

Partech Ventures
Gipsstraße 3
10119 Berlin
partechpartners.com

Paua Ventures Verwaltungs GmbH
Schicklerstraße 5-7
10179 Berlin
pauaventures.com

Project A Ventures
Julie-Wolfthorn-Straße 1
10115 Berlin
project-a.com

Point Nine Capital
Chausseestraße 19
10115 Berlin
pointninecap.com

signals
Am Nordbahnhof 3
10115 Berlin
hellosignals.com

Target Global
Schinkelplatz 5
10117 Berlin
targetglobal.vc

Torch Partners
Kastanienallee 76
10435 Berlin
torchpartners.com

Westtech Ventures
4th floor, Building 12/1
Voltastraße 6
13355 Berlin
westtechventures.de

Language Schools

Babylonia e.V.
Cuvrystraße 23a
10997 Berlin
babylonia.de

die deutSCHule
Karl-Marx-Straße 107
12043 Berlin
die-deutschule.de

Die Berliner Volkshochschulen
berlin.de/vhs

DSB - DeutschAkademie Sprachschule Berlin GmbH
Bayreutherstraße 8
10787 Berlin
deutschakademie.de

Expath
Torstr. 117
10119 Berlin
expath.de

GLS German Language School c/o GLS Campus Berlin
Kastanienallee 82
10435 Berlin
gls-berlin.de

Goethe-Institut Berlin
Neue Schönhauserstraße 20
10178 Berlin
goethe.de

Speakeasy Sprachzeug
Warschauer Straße 36
10243 Berlin
speakeasysprachzeug.de

Sprachmafia
Schillerpromenade 25
12049 Berlin
sprachmafia.com

Sprachsalon Berlin
Weichselstraße 38
12045 Berlin
sprachsalon-berlin.de

Startup Events

12min.me Berlin
meetup.com/12minB

betabreakfast
betahaus.com/event/betabreakfast

Berlin Demo Day by START Berlin
berlindemoday.de

Berlin Startup Employees Meet Up
facebook.com/groups/berlin-startups/

Berlin Talent Summit
talentsummit.co

Creative Mornings
creativemornings.com/cities/ber

CUBE Tech Fair
cube-global.com

Data Natives
datanatives.io

EventHorizon
eventhorizon2018.com

Factory Berlin Events
factoryberlin.com/events

Fuckup Nights
fuckupnights.com

HEUREKA
heureka-conference.com

NOAH Berlin
noah-conference.com/noah-berlin-2017

Republica
re-publica.com

Silicon Allee Monthly Meetup
meetup.com/Silicon-Allee-Events

Silicon Drinkabout Berlin
meetup.com/Silicon-Drinkabout-Berlin

Startup Camp
scb18.de

Startup Grind
startupgrind.com/berlin

Startup Safari
berlin.startupsafari.com

Startupnight
startupnight.net

Tech Open Air
toa.berlin

TYPO talks
typotalks.com/berlin

Quo Vadis
qvconf.com

glossary

A

Accelerator
An organization or program that offers advice and resources to help small businesses grow

Acqui-hire
Buying out a company based on the skills of its staff rather than its service or product

Angel Investment
Outside funding with shared ownership equity

ARR
Accounting (or average) rate of return: calculation generated from net income of the proposed capital investment

B

B2B (Business-to-Business)
The exchange of services, information and/or products from a business to a business

B2C (Business-to-Consumer)
The exchange of services, information and/or products from a business to a consumer

BOM (Bill of Materials)
The list of the parts or components required to build a product

Bootstrap
To self-fund, without outside investment

Bridge Loan
A short-term loan taken out from between two weeks and three years pending arrangement of longer-term financing

Burn Rate
The amount of money a startup spends

Business Angel
An experienced entrepreneur or professional who provides starting or growth capital for promising startups

C

C-level
Chief position

Canvas Business Model
A template for developing new or documenting existing business models

Cap Table
An analysis of the founders' and investors' percentage of ownership, equity dilution and value of equity in each round of investment

CMO
Chief marketing officer

Cold-Calling
The solicitation of potential customers who were not anticipating such an interaction

Convertible Note/Loan
A type of short-term debt often used by seed investors to delay establishing a valuation for the startup until a later round of funding or milestone

Coworking
A shared working environment

CPA
Cost per action

CPC
Cost per click

Cybersecurity
The body of technologies, processes and practices designed to protect networks, computers, programs and data from attack, damage or unauthorized access

D

Dealflow
Term for investors to refer to the rate at which they receive business proposals

Deeptech
Companies founded on a scientific discovery or meaningful engineering innovation

Diluting
A reduction in the ownership percentage of a share of stock caused by the issuance of new shares

E

Elevator Pitch
A short summary used to quickly define a product or idea

Exit
A way to transition the ownership of a company to another company

F

Fintech
Financial technology

Flex Desk
Shared desk in a space where coworkers are free to move around and sit wherever they like

I

Incubator
Facility established to nurture young startup firms during their early months or years

Installed Base
A reliable indicator of a platform's popularity

IP (Intellectual Property)
Intangible property that is the result of creativity, such as patents, copyrights, etc

IPO (Initial Public Offering)
The first time a company's stock is offered for sale to the public

K

KPI (Key Performance Indicator)
A measurable value that demonstrates how effectively a company is achieving key business objectives

L

Later-Stage
More mature startups/ companies

Lean
Refers to 'lean startup methodology;' the method proposed by Eric Ries in his book for developing businesses and startups through product development cycles

M

M&A (Mergers and Acquisitions)
A merger is a combination of two companies to form a new company, while an acquisition is the purchase of one company by another in which no new company is formed

MAU
Monthly active user

MVP
Minimum viable product

P

P2P (Peer-to-Peer)
A network created when two or more PCs are connected and sharing resources without going through a separate server

Pitch Deck
A short version of a business plan presenting key figures

PR-Kit (Press Kit)
Package of pictures, logos and descriptions of your services

Pro-market
A market economy/a capitalistic economy

R

Runtime
The amount of time a startup has survived

S

SaaS
Software as a service

Scaleup
Company that has already validated its product in a market, and is economically sustainable

Seed Funding
First round, small, early-stage investment from family members, friends, banks or an investor

Seed Investor
An investor focusing on the seed round

Seed Round
The first round of funding

Series A/B/C/D
The name of funding rounds coming after the seed stage

Shares
The amount of the company that belongs to someone

Solopreneurs
somebody developing their own personal brand; not a company to hire employees

Startup
Companies under three years old, in the growth stage and becoming profitable (if not already)

SVP
Senior Vice President

T

Term Sheet/Letter of Intent
The document between an investor and a startup including the conditions for financing (commonly non-binding)

U

Unicorn
A company worth over US$1 billion

USP
unique selling point

UX (User experience design)
The process of enhancing user satisfaction by improving the usability, accessibility and pleasure provided in the interaction between the user and the product

V

VC (Venture Capital)
Outside venture capital investment from a pool of investors in a venture capital firm in return for equity

Vesting
Employee rights to employer-provided assets over time, which gives the employee an incentive to perform well and remain with the company

→ startupguide.world

Follow us

About the Guide

Based on traditional guidebooks that can be carried around everywhere, Startup Guide books help you navigate and connect with different startup scenes across the globe. Each book is packed with useful information, exciting entrepreneur stories and insightful interviews with local experts. As the world of work changes, our mission is to guide, empower and inspire people to start their own business anywhere. We hope the book will become your trusted companion as you embark on a new (startup) journey. Today, Startup Guide books are in 17 different cities in Europe and the Middle East, including Berlin, London, Tel Aviv, Stockholm, Copenhagen, Vienna, Lisbon and Paris.

How we make the guides:
To ensure an accurate and trustworthy guide every time, we team up with a city partner that is established in the local startup scene. Then we ask the local community to nominate startups, co-working spaces, founders, incubators and established businesses to be featured through an online submission form. Based on the results, these submissions are narrowed down to the top fifty companies and individuals. Afterwards, the local advisory board – which is selected by our community partner and consists of key players in the local startup community – votes for the final selection so there's a balanced representation of industries and startup stories in each book. The local community partner then works in close collaboration with our editorial and design team in Berlin to help research, organize interviews with journalists as well as plan photoshoots with photographers. Finally, all content is reviewed, edited and put into the book's layout by the Startup Guide team in Berlin and Lisbon before going for print in Berlin.

Where to find us: The easiest way to get your hands on a Startup Guide book is to order it from our online shop: **startupguide.world/shop**
If you prefer to do things in real life, drop by one of the fine retailers listed on the stockists page on our website.

Want to become a stockist or suggest a store?

Get in touch here:
sales@startupguide.world

STARTUP
GUIDE
STORE

The Startup Guide Stores

Whether it's sniffing freshly printed books or holding an innovative product, we're huge fans of physical experiences. That's why we opened two stores–one in Lisbon another in Berlin. Not only do the stores showcase our books and curated products, they're also our offices and a place for the community to come together to share wows and hows. Say hello!

Lisbon:
R. Rodrigues de Faria 103
Edifício G6, 1300 - 501 Lisboa
Tue-Sun: 12h-19h
+351 21 139 8791
lisbon@startupguide.world

Berlin:
Waldemarstraße 38, 10999 Berlin
Mon-Fri: 10h-18h
+49 (0)30-37468679
berlin@startupguide.world

#startupeverywhere

Startup Guide is a creative content and publishing company founded by Sissel Hansen in 2014. We produce guidebooks and tools to help entrepreneurs navigate and connect with different startup scenes across the globe. As the world of work changes, our mission is to guide, empower and inspire people to start their own business anywhere. Today, Startup Guide books are in 17 different cities in Europe and the Middle East, including Berlin, London, Tel Aviv, Stockholm, Copenhagen, Vienna, Lisbon and Paris. We also have two physical stores in Berlin and Lisbon to promote and sell products by startup. Startup Guide is a 20-person team based in Berlin and Lisbon.
Visit our site for more: startupguide.world

Want to get more info, be a partner or say hello?

Shoot us an email here info@startupguide.world

Join us and #startupeverywhere

With thanks to our **content sponsors**

Google for Entrepreneurs

INNOVATION HUB

FLEET BOARD

signals

TAB

With thanks to our **Community Partner**

Silicon Allee

Event Partner / Tech Open Air - The Future of Tech, Work and Life

This June 19–22, Tech Open Air (TOA) will throw open its doors to twenty thousand attendees all eager to learn about the future of music, art, tech and science. This unique four-day technology festival held at the iconic Funkhaus Berlin provides a platform for entrepreneurs to engage with change-makers from across the globe. Over 150 speakers – including Daniel Miller (founder of Mute Records), Stefan Thomas (CTO, Ripple), Lily Peng (researcher at Google) and Boyan Slat (The Ocean Cleanup) – will share their insights about where they see the world evolving and explore how we can use technology to better harness and understand these changes.

TOA's epic Haus of Tech exhibition space will play host to the likes of Daimler, Google and T-Systems alongside leading executives and companies, taking to the innovation stage. This year's biggest startup competition, the Digital Top 50 Awards, will showcase promising scaleups pitching and competing for a huge selection of prizes in front of leading CxOs worldwide. Among the judges will be the CTO of Siemens, the VP of Marketing at Google, and the Head of APAC at IBM.

In addition to the two-day conference program, TOA is hosting 120+ satellite events all around the city, transforming Berlin into an interactive hub for interdisciplinary events. From rooftop yoga to hackathons, and workshops to boat parties, the hottest companies will be placing their unique stamp on TOA and offering networking opportunities for everyone.

For the first time this year, TOA has also partnered with MeetFrank, the secret recruitment app, to bring you the crème de la crème in tech talent. Get exclusive access to high-level professionals currently employed elsewhere, set up interviews, and recruit your future employees over a beer by the Spree.

If you're looking to recruit or be recruited, then TOA is the place to be this summer. Join us and learn from the best while networking and collaborating with thought leaders worldwide. TOA18 offers a truly one-of-a-kind experience to future-proof your life and business this year.

Visit: toa.berlin for more info.

[Links] Facebook: **TechOpenAir** Twitter: **@TOABerlin** Instagram: **toaberlin**

How
Much
Is
I Am The
Horseman
VOLVO

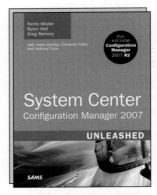

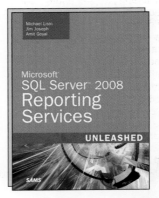

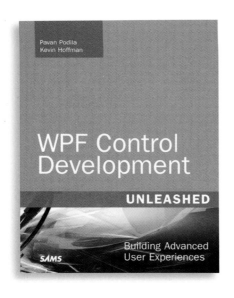

STARTUP GUIDE BERLIN

In partnership with **Silicon Allee**

STARTUP GUIDE BERLIN

Startup Guide Berlin V.4

EDITORIAL
Publisher: Sissel Hansen
Editor: Marissa van Uden
Proofreader: Ted Hermann
Contributing Editor: Charmaine Li
Staff Writers: Josh Raisher, Mark Fletcher, Charmaine Li, Jesse Van Mouwerik, John Sperryn, Alex Gerald
Contributing Writers: Michelle Arrouas, L Isaac Simon, Lars Mensel

PRODUCTION
Head of Production: Tim Rhodes
Researchers: Eglė Duleckytė, İrem Topçuoğlu, Andrew Haw

DESIGN & PHOTOGRAPHY
Designer: Ines Pedro
Photographer: Daniela Carducci

Additional photography by
Ryan Song, Hoffotografen, Dominik Tryba, Moritz Jekat, Jasmin Schuller, Berlin Partner- Photostudio Charlottenburg, Gorazd Rutar, Dara Francis Elie, Dan Taylor, Stefan Kny and Unsplash.com

Illustrations by Joana Carvalho

SALES & DISTRIBUTION
Head of Sales: Marlene do Vale marlene@startupguide.world
Head of Community Growth: Eglė Duleckytė egle@startupguide.world
Head of Business Development: Anna Weissensteiner anna@startupguide.world
Head of Distribution: İrem Topçuoğlu irem@startupguide.world

Printed in Berlin, Germany by
Medialis-Offsetdruck GmbH
Heidelbergerstraße 65, 12435 Berlin

Published by Startup Guide World IVS
Kanonbådsvej 2, 1437 Copenhagen K

info@startupguide.world
Visit us: startupguide.world
@StartupGuideHQ

ISBN: 978-3-947624-07-2

GW00992203

STARTUP GUIDE

#startupeverywhere